Writing mechanics

Year 6

Rachel Clarke

About this book

Grammar is at the heart of communication. Every sentence that we read, speak or write is structured through the rules of grammar. With practice, most pupils can recognise grammatical structures in short questions, like those in the Spelling, Grammar and Punctuation test. What they find harder to do is to use those grammatical structures effectively and accurately in their own writing.

To help pupils use grammar effectively in their writing, we need to offer them opportunities to use grammatical structures authentically. That is, we need to think about where different grammatical structures are used in order to effectively communicate the purpose of a text with its intended audience.

Authenticity is central to the approach in this book. Authenticity is not about giving pupils a tick list of grammatical features to squeeze into a piece of writing. It's about knowing and recognising where and when grammatical features are used in effective writing. It's an approach where teachers select a purpose and audience for pupils' writing that enables learning of key grammatical features. For example, a teacher wanting pupils to understand command sentences might scrutinise instruction writing, whereas a teacher looking to teach the subjunctive form might look at texts about wishes and aspirations. It's an approach that puts the grammar listed in the National Curriculum first.

Each unit in this book begins with an example text. Through reading the text with pupils, the purpose (whether it is written to explain, instruct, argue, etc.) and audience (parents, children, people interested in a specific topic, etc.) can be established.

The unit then focuses on identifying one or more of the grammatical features that support the purpose and audience of the text. Through the use of creative activities, each unit then provides opportunities to build confidence with the grammatical features. Finally, through modelled and demonstration writing, the book offers scaffolded opportunities for pupils to write their own texts using the grammatical features they have learned about.

Each unit in this book recognises that pupils work at different rates and so independent tasks, support tasks and extension tasks are included. Teachers may choose to use all, or some, of these activities to meet the varying needs of pupils across the class. Whichever approach is taken, each activity is designed to prepare pupils for writing their own texts using the grammatical features covered in the unit.

Editing, improving and proof-reading skills are covered in each unit through the use of model texts. In these sessions pupils are asked to compare and evaluate different model texts, to proof-read for punctuation errors and to improve model texts in preparation for writing their own texts.

Many of the activities in the book are based around resource sheets for pupils to complete. Small versions of the sheets are included in the book for reference. Full-size versions are provided on the Keen Kite website. There are also sections of text that need to be displayed for pupils to see. This text is highlighted in the book and is also available on the Keen Kite website. All of this content can be downloaded from collins.co.uk/keenkite/downloads

Contents

Learning outcome: to write poetry using synonyms and antonyms as cohesive devices

Keywords: cohesion, derivation, repetition, comparative adjective, pronoun, synonym, antonym

BLACK HOLES

What are black holes?

Black holes aren't actually holes. They don't lead anywhere – you can't go through a black hole and end up somewhere else.

A black hole is more like a tiny, invisible point in space, which works like a powerful plughole. Objects that come close to a black hole get pulled towards it, then disappear into it – whether they're very small, like dust, or large, like rocks. Black holes can even swallow whole moons, planets and stars. If a spaceship flew too close to a black hole, it would get pulled in too. So would you, if you were floating past in a spacesuit.

Black holes are small but dense

All the stuff that gets sucked into a black hole is compressed into a tiny dot in the middle. That dot is smaller than a grape. It's smaller than a grain of sand. In fact, it's so small it takes up no space at all!

If you could hold a black hole in your hand, it would be invisible, yet heavier than the Sun. The Sun weighs about 2,000,000,000,000,000,000,000,000,000,000 kilograms. That's 300,000 times more than Earth and 30 billion times more than you!

So how can something so small have such strong gravity? Black holes have strong gravity because they're very dense. Density means how heavy something is for its size.

A piece of packaging foam is very light. But a piece of gold exactly the same size is very heavy. This is because gold is denser than foam. It has more stuff packed into the same amount of space.

Earth is quite dense. It's mostly made of rock and metal, which is very heavy for its size. But black holes are even denser. They are much smaller than Earth, but they are much heavier. In fact, they are the densest objects in the universe.

How do you find a black hole?

Space scientists look for black holes using telescopes. But how do you find something so tiny and invisible in space? Each black hole has a ball-shaped area around it. Within the ball-shaped area, nothing can escape from its gravity. This area is much bigger than the black hole itself.

Once something has passed into the ball-shaped area around a black hole, it can't be seen. But space scientists can see objects such as stars orbiting around the ball-shaped area and changing shape as they are pulled towards the black hole. The black hole's powerful gravity makes stars stretch out into a string, like a lump of modelling clay when you pull on it.

As objects pass close to a black hole, its gravity may make them change direction. If they get close enough, they spiral around the black hole as they get sucked in, like water swirling down a plughole. The objects move faster and faster as they get closer to the middle. When space scientists see this "plughole effect" happening in space, it means they may have found a black hole.

If you half-fill a sink with water, add glitter to the water and then pull the plug out, the glitter will spiral around the plughole, going faster and faster as it gets closer to the middle. A black hole works the same way.

Sometimes, a star is near a black hole, but not close enough to get sucked in. The black hole and the star pull on each other and orbit around each other. So if a space scientist sees a star circling around something they can't see, this can tell them where a black hole is hiding.

Black holes are also thought to send out streams of X-rays, which are a kind of energy ray, similar to light. We can't see X-rays ourselves, but we have telescopes that can detect them. So this is another clue that can show where in space black holes are.

Black Holes by Anna Claybourne

Links to the National Curriculum

Reading – comprehension

- maintain positive attitudes to reading and understanding of what they read by continuing to read and discuss an increasingly wide range of fiction, poetry, plays, non-fiction and reference books or textbooks
- understand what they read by identifying how language, structure and presentation contribute to meaning

Writing – composition

- plan their writing by identifying the audience for and purpose of the writing, selecting the appropriate form and using other similar writing as models for their own
- perform their own compositions, using appropriate intonation, volume, and movement so that meaning is clear

Writing – vocabulary, grammar and punctuation

- understand how words are related by meaning as synonyms and antonyms

Reading the text

1 session

Reading for meaning

Provide pupils with a copy of the extract and read it aloud with them. Ask them to identify the subject of the extract (black holes), the genre (information text) and the purpose of the text (to inform and explain). Ask pupils to reread the extract, identifying any words they are unsure of. If they are unable to use the context to work out the meanings of these words, they should circle them. Talk about the words pupils have circled, providing definitions where necessary.

Ask pupils why they think the author has compared objects getting sucked into black holes to water swirling around a plughole. Listen to their responses, clarifying that it is unlikely that the reader will have seen a black hole so comparing them to something they have experienced makes the text easier to understand. Ask pupils to explain what is meant by 'density' (how heavy something is for its size). Encourage them to explain how the author has helped readers understand this difficult concept (by describing and comparing the density of two familiar objects: packing foam and gold).

Reading for grammar

Explain that pupils will be looking at how the author has created cohesion in order to write their own cohesive poems.

Ask pupils to reread the section *'How do you find a black hole?'*, noting how many times the author has written 'black hole' (18). Ask why they think the author has repeated this phrase (because black holes are what the text is about). Now ask them to count the frequency of the phrase 'ball-shaped' (4). Explain that the repetition of 'ball-shaped' secures an important idea in the reader's mind, helping them to understand the text. Explain that repetition is a useful way to create cohesion in a text.

Ask pupils to reread the section *'Black holes are small but dense'* and to find the sentence defining 'density' ('Density means how heavy something is for its size.'). Challenge them to find other derivatives of 'dense' in this section (denser, densest). Explain to pupils that using derivatives of a word in this way creates cohesion in a text.

Draw a word web using dense, denser, densest and density. For example:

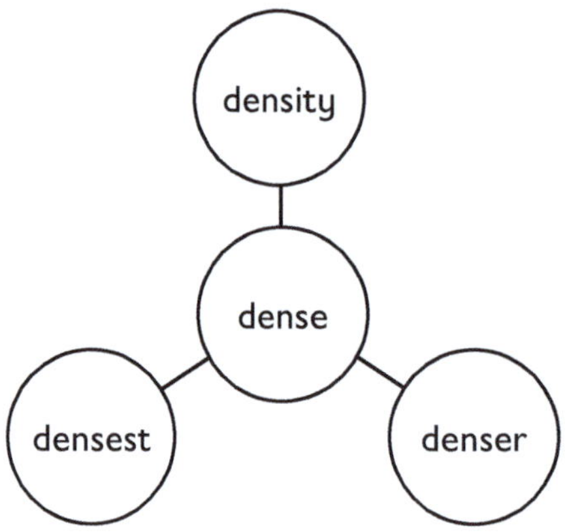

Ask pupils to use dictionaries to create word webs for heavy (heavier, heaviest); pull (pulls, pulling, pulled); gravity (gravitate/s, gravitational, gravitating); compressed (compress/es, compression, compressing). Check their word webs for accuracy and challenge pupils to write sentences using the words.

Independent task

Ask pupils to reread the section *'How do you find a black hole?'* Discuss the author's use of 'orbiting around', and how it means moving around an object in a curving path. Ask pupils to reread the section, highlighting phrases with meanings similar to 'orbiting around' (spiral around, circling around). Explain that using synonyms within a text is a cohesive device that creates interest and avoids over-repetition of the same word.

Distribute copies of the resource sheet *Substituting synonyms*. Explain to pupils that they are going to rewrite the sentences by substituting a synonym for the underlined words. For example:

I really love my dog. → I really adore my dog.

Remind them to use a thesaurus to help them with this activity.

Resource sheet: Substituting synonyms

1. We learned new skills in football practice this week.
2. I shattered the window when I accidentally threw the ball at it.
3. The wolf bared its teeth. It looked fierce.
4. Rapunzel let down her beautiful hair for the prince to climb up.
5. I was feeling under the weather, so mum said I could stay off school.
6. All their belongings packed, they set off on an adventure.

Early finishers should find synonyms for the following words and use them in sentences: run, big, scary, nice, kind.

Support task

Distribute a set of the cards from the resource sheet *Synonym match* to each pair of pupils. Ask pupils to shuffle the cards and then find the bold words. Explain that there are three synonyms for each bold word and ask them to work with their partner to match the bold cards with the correct synonyms. Remind pupils to use a thesaurus to check their answers. Early finishers should write sentences using the synonyms they matched.

Resource sheet: Synonym match

love	cherish	adore	treasure
hate	loathe	detest	despise
walk	stride	wander	stroll
sleep	slumber	doze	snooze
house	home	dwelling	residence
hungry	starving	ravenous	famished

Extension task

Ask pupils to tell you the opposite term to synonym (antonym). Explain that antonyms can be used cohesively to show contrast and to provide wide-ranging descriptions. Ask pupils to reread the section '*What are black holes?*', locating where the author has used two antonyms ('whether they're very small, like dust, or large, like rocks'). Ask them to discuss why the author has done this. Listen to their responses, clarifying that by using these antonyms, the author has shown the power of black holes as they act on everything regardless of size.

Ask pupils to write the following words in their workbook and to use a thesaurus to find antonyms for each:

ancient (e.g. modern); artificial (e.g. natural); bitter (e.g. sweet); coarse (e.g. fine); deep (e.g. shallow); good (e.g. evil); poverty (e.g. wealth); rapid (e.g. slow); vague (e.g. clear)

When they have finished, they should write sentences for each pair of antonyms. For example:

In Shanghai, <u>ancient</u> buildings stand side-by-side with <u>modern</u> ones, creating a stunning view.

Evaluating and improving writing 1 session

Distribute copies of the resource sheet *The planets*. Ask pupils to read the sheet. Explain that they should think about how to fill in the gaps by using synonyms, antonyms and derivatives of words to ensure that it makes sense and is cohesive. When they have filled in all of the gaps, they should consider whether they have made the most effective choice (e.g. would orbit be more effective than circle?). Pupils should also consider using pronouns to replace the repeated use of the planets' names, and how some sentences could be combined to make the passage flow more easily.

Resource sheet: The planets

<u>The planets</u>

There are nine planets in our Solar System. At the ________________ of the Solar System is the Sun. The nine planets ________________ around the Sun. We describe this motion of circling around the Sun as an orbit.

Mercury is the smallest planet and it is the ________________ to the Sun. It takes 88 days for Mercury to ________________ around the Sun. After Mercury comes Venus. Venus is about the same size as Earth and, like Earth, it has an atmosphere. But Venus is too hot to live on. In fact, it is ________________ than Mercury even though Mercury is ________________ to the Sun.

The next planet in the Solar System is Earth. Earth is the only planet known to have life. Earth has a small satellite called the moon. This ________________ around Earth. It takes about 28 days to complete this ________________ motion. After Earth comes Mars. Mars is not as big as Earth or Venus. Mars is sometimes called the Red Planet as its surface is covered in red rocks. It takes Mars 687 days to ________________ the Sun.

Next comes Jupiter. It is the ________________ planet in the Solar System. It is so large that its mass is 2 ½ times that of all the other planets in the Solar System put together. Jupiter takes 12 years to ________________ the Sun.

The sixth planet from the Sun is Saturn. Saturn is not quite as large as Jupiter. It has rings and it has over 60 satellites.

It takes 29 years to orbit the Sun. The last three planets of the Solar System are Uranus, Neptune and Pluto. Scientists now think that Pluto is a dwarf planet and part of a system of other dwarf planets called the Kuiper belt. The Kuiper belt is a huge collection of dwarf planets, asteroids, ice and dust that ________________ the Sun on the edges of the Solar System.

Grammar in action: writing poetry using synonyms and antonyms 1 session

Explain to pupils that they are going to write a pair of poems using synonyms and antonyms. Ask pupils to think of words associated with poverty and wealth, using a thesaurus to help them. Listen to their responses, adding your own suggestions if necessary, and organise them into nouns, adjectives, verbs and adverbs.

Display the poem structure shown on the resource sheet *Poverty and Wealth poems* and explain to pupils that they will use this structure to write their own poems. Demonstrate how to use this structure to write a pair of poems, using the example on the sheet.

- Demonstrate using a thesaurus to choose adjectives to describe poverty. For example, start by writing 'needy' and 'broke' and then model changing them to 'poor' and 'penniless', explaining that these synonyms create an alliterative pattern in the poem.
- Discuss how repeating '-ing' in the second line of each poem creates a cohesive pattern.
- Ask pupils to consider the effectiveness of the fourth line of the two poems. They should note that they are synonyms for the title of each poem. You may want to use a thesaurus to explore these words as 'plenty' can be used as a noun, quantifier and adverb.
- Ask pupils to consider what makes the poems cohesive, clarifying that they begin and end with synonyms and all lines refer to the characteristics of poverty and wealth through the use of words with similar meanings. Pupils should also note that the pair of poems are opposites.
- Review the punctuation in the poems. You may want to start with a version of the poems without 'end of line' punctuation and then consider the effectiveness of adding the commas to separate the list of descriptions and the semi-colons to bind the descriptions to the final word.

Ask pupils to write their own pair of poems, choosing antonyms that are either concrete or abstract nouns (e.g. day and night, courage and cowardice, good and bad). Encourage them to edit and improve their compositions, checking that they have followed the given structure. They should be encouraged to read their finished poems to the rest of the class.

Resource sheet: Poverty and Wealth poems

Poem structure

1. A noun
2. Two adjectives
3. Three words ending in 'ing'
4. Four-word phrase about the object/how it makes you feel
5. A noun – synonym of the first line

Poverty
Poor, penniless,
Wanting, needing, hoping,
Opportunities out of reach;
Hardship.

Wealth
Rich, prosperous,
Spending, getting, having,
A world of possibilities;
Plenty.

Learning outcome: to use the passive voice and cohesive devices to write an explanatory text

Keywords: authentic, purpose, audience, auxiliary verb, past participle, passive voice, cohesion

FABULOUS BRIDGES

EARLY BRIDGES

People have been building bridges across rivers and valleys for thousands of years. Cut-down trees bridged narrow streams, rope bridges spanned wider valleys and raised walkways crossed marshes. As people learned more, they were able to build bigger bridges to carry more weight, and longer bridges to cross wider gaps.

Roman arches

Bridges were built in ancient Egypt and Greece. But the real experts in bridge building in the ancient world were the Romans, who came later. Some of their bridges are still standing, nearly 2,000 years after they were built. The Romans discovered a waterproof concrete, called pozzolana. This building material helped them to build strong bridge supports, or **piers**, in rivers. Using these piers, Romans built road bridges as well as bridges called **aqueducts** for carrying water.

Building from iron

Stone was the usual material for building big bridges until the 18th century. When a bridge was needed to span the River Severn in England, designers decided to build it from iron instead of stone. Called the Iron Bridge, this was the world's first bridge made of iron. In total, the bridge is 60 metres in length. Its longest span is 30.5 metres long. The village alongside the bridge was named Ironbridge.

BROOKLYN BRIDGE

The Brooklyn Bridge is one of the most familiar landmarks of New York City. This suspension bridge links Manhattan with Brooklyn over the East River.

Building the towers

The bridge's **deck** hangs from cables that pass over the top of the two towers. These towers, which stand in the river, were built with deep **foundations**. Digging these was a difficult and dangerous job. A huge box called a **caisson** was lowered to the river bed where each tower was to stand. Builders climbed down into a chamber at the bottom of each caisson and dug out the mud and rock. Then the caissons were filled with concrete and the masonry towers were built above them.

Father and son

Brooklyn Bridge was designed by John A. Roebling, who died from an infection before construction began. His son, Washington Roebling, who was a **civil engineer**, took over. However, he suffered a serious accident and was confined to his bed. He ran the rest of the project from home, watching work on the bridge through a telescope.

SYDNEY HARBOUR BRIDGE

Sydney Harbour Bridge is a steel arch bridge that spans the narrowest part of Sydney Harbour. It was modelled on the smaller Hell Gate Bridge in New York City, built in 1916. The deck, or flat surface, of an arched bridge is usually above the arch. Sydney Harbour Bridge is different. Its deck hangs below the 503-metre arch. Because of its shape, this famous Australian bridge is known as 'The Coathanger'.

Granite towers

Each half of Sydney Harbour Bridge's massive arch was built out from the shore towards the middle. Cables anchored to the ground stopped the two halves from falling into the sea until they met in the middle. Then the roadway was added and the stone towers, called **pylons**, were built at each end. The pylons hold the ends of the arch firmly in position.

Red-hot rivets

Most of the steel used to build Sydney Harbour Bridge was made in England and shipped halfway around the world to Sydney. The granite was quarried at Moruya on the south coast of New South Wales in Australia. The steel parts were lifted into position and fastened together with pins called rivets. These rivets were heated until they were red-hot, then thrown up to rivet catchers on the bridge who hammered them in place.

GLOSSARY

aqueduct bridge that carries water across a valley

caisson large tank, open at the bottom, used to build bridge foundations. A caisson is sunk to the river bed. Water is pumped out. Workmen enter the caisson and dig down until they reach solid rock. Then the caisson is filled with concrete to form the foundation of one of the bridge's piers

civil engineer an engineer who works primarily with construction projects in public places. These include office buildings, bridges and roads

deck part of a bridge that cars or trains are driven along

foundations solid underground structure on which a building, such as a bridge, stands. A bridge's foundations always extend many metres below ground

pier one of the supports that bears the weight of a bridge

pylons tall towers that support a bridge's cables or arch

Fabulous Bridges by Ian Graham

Links to the National Curriculum

Reading – comprehension

- discuss and evaluate how authors use language, including figurative language, considering the impact on the reader
- retrieve, record and present information from non-fiction

Writing – composition

- plan their writing by identifying the audience for and purpose of the writing, selecting the appropriate form and using other similar writing as models for their own
- draft and write by selecting appropriate grammar and vocabulary, understanding how such choices can change and enhance meaning
- draft and write by using a wide range of devices to build cohesion within and across paragraphs
- evaluate and edit by proposing changes to vocabulary, grammar and punctuation to enhance effects and clarify meaning

Writing – vocabulary, grammar and punctuation

- use passive verbs to affect the presentation of information in a sentence

TEACHING AND LEARNING IDEAS

Reading the text

1 session

Reading for meaning

Provide pupils with a copy of the extract. Read aloud with pupils, modelling how to use the glossary to check the meaning of the words in bold. Ask pupils to reread the extract and identify any further words they are unsure about. Provide definitions as required.

Monitor pupils' understanding of the text by asking questions about the extract, e.g. What type of bridge is the Brooklyn Bridge? (suspension) Which section tells you about the first bridge built from iron? *('Building from iron')* Why do you think the Sydney Harbour Bridge spans the narrowest part of Sydney Harbour? (It was easier to build it here; it would use fewer materials than if it bridged a wider part of the harbour.) Discuss pupils' responses, encouraging them to show the location of the answers. Show them an image of the Sydney Harbour Bridge and a coathanger and ask them to consider whether this is an appropriate nickname for the bridge.

Reading for grammar

Ask pupils to identify the extract's purpose (explanation / information text) and intended audience (people interested in bridges). Explain that they will be learning about the grammatical features used by the author so that they can write their own effective explanation text.

Introduce the term 'passive voice', explaining that this type of text is usually created by using the auxiliary verb 'be' (am, are, be, been, being, is, was, were), plus the past participle -ing for present tense verbs and -ed for past tense verbs, although there are many exceptions such as 'written' and 'eaten'.

Write the following examples on the whiteboard:

A local celebrity *presented* the prize. (active)

The prize *was presented* by a local celebrity. (passive)

Draw pupils' attention to the use of the verb 'be' (*was*) and the use of the past participle *presented* in the second sentence. Explain that in the first sentence the focus is on the celebrity making the presentation and in the second sentence the focus is on the prize. Explain that this is what the passive voice does: it makes active verbs like *presented* passive.

Now draw the pupils' attention to the phrase 'by a' in the second sentence. Explain that 'by / by the / by a' are sometimes, **but not always**, used in passive sentences.

Ask pupils to write 'active' on one side of a mini whiteboard and 'passive' on the other. Explain that they are going to practise recognising active and passive structures. Dictate sentences and ask pupils to show the appropriate side of their whiteboard in response. Example sentences could include:

Joe drove the car. (active)	The car was driven by Joe. (passive)
Sarah read the book in one day. (active)	The book was read in one day by Sarah. (passive)
Mo hid the treasure. (active)	The treasure was hidden by Mo. (passive)
The rain drenched everyone. (active)	Everyone was drenched by the rain. (passive)
Flo sent Sam a Valentine card. (active)	The Valentine card was sent to Sam. (passive)

You may need to explain that the last example is passive but that the person performing the action in the sentence (Flo) has been left out. Writing the sentence as 'The Valentine card was sent to Sam by Flo' may help your explanation.

Return to the extract. Read from the beginning of the extract to the end of the section '*Building the towers*'. As you read, ask pupils to underline examples of the passive voice. For example:

Bridges <u>were built</u> in ancient Egypt and Greece … These towers, which stand in the river, <u>were built</u> with deep foundations … A huge box called a caisson <u>was lowered</u> … Then the caissons <u>were filled</u> … the masonry towers <u>were built</u> …

Independent task

Provide pupils with a copy of the extract. Ask them to work with a partner to locate and highlight further examples of the passive voice in the text. When they have finished, review the extract with them, noting that the passive voice has been formed in this extract without the use of the 'by / by the / by a' tag. Discuss how explanatory texts often use the passive voice as it puts the emphasis on what is being explained rather than on who or what is undertaking the actions. Early finishers should write some passive sentences of their own in their workbook.

Support task

Provide pupils with the sentences from the resource sheet *Active or passive?* and ask them to sort them into active and passive. Before starting the task, teach pupils how to test if a sentence is active or passive by adding 'by / by the / by a' and a noun phrase to the end of the sentence: if it makes sense when this is added, it is usually passive. If it doesn't make sense with the addition, it is usually active. This can be made more fun by assigning characters to undertake the actions, such as monsters or unicorns. For example:

The glass in the greenhouse was broken *(by monsters)*. The addition of 'by monsters' makes sense (they are performing the action in the sentence). The sentence is passive.

The dog caught the stick *(by monsters)*. The addition of 'by monsters' doesn't make sense (the dog is already performing the action in the sentence). The sentence is active.

Resource sheet: Active or passive?

Active	Passive
Sydney Harbour Bridge is a steel arch bridge that spans the narrowest part of Sydney Harbour.	Bridges were built by the ancient Greeks, the Egyptians and the Romans.
Builders climbed into the caissons so they could build the foundations of the Brooklyn Bridge.	The Iron Bridge was constructed in the 18th century.
The Iron Bridge crosses the River Severn.	The towers of the Brooklyn Bridge were built with deep foundations.
Washington Roebling managed the construction of the Brooklyn Bridge after the death of his father.	Huge pylons were added to the Sydney Harbour Bridge.
The Brooklyn Bridge is one of the most familiar landmarks of New York City.	New bridges are being built all over the world.

Extension task

Read or display the following questions and ask pupils to identify which use the active and which use the passive voice:

1. What was the name of the waterproof material discovered by the Romans?
2. Up to the 1900s, what was used to build most bridges?
3. What type of bridge is the Brooklyn Bridge?
4. What are pylons?

Ask pupils to write 10 quiz questions based on '*Fabulous Bridges*' using the passive voice. When they have written their questions, they should swap with another pupil and answer each other's questions.

As an extra challenge, consider asking the most able pupils if any of their responses were in the passive voice. For example, 'Up to the 1900s, stone was used to build most bridges'.

Provide pupils with copies of the resource sheet *Building the towers.*

Ask them to work in pairs to compare the two passages. They should evaluate which they think is the most effective, giving reasons to support their opinions.

Listen to their thoughts, explaining, if necessary, that the first passage overuses the noun phrase 'the two towers' and that most sentences in the first passage also begin with a noun phrase (the bridge's deck; the two towers; a huge box; the caissons). Ask pupils to describe what they think makes the second passage better / worse than the first one. Clarify their responses, referring to the following points which create cohesion across the second paragraph:

- ***These towers,*** – the use of the pronoun 'these' immediately after 'the two towers' at the end of the previous sentence binds the two sentences together, signalling that the second sentence is going to add further information about the towers.
- ***which stand in the river*** – the relative pronoun 'which' creates a relative clause that adds further information about the position of the towers.
- ***these*** – this time, 'these' is being used to refer to the foundations. The author has used the same technique as before, placing the pronoun near the beginning of the sentence to connect it to the noun (foundations).
- ***each tower was*** – the use of 'each' (as a determiner in this example) tells the reader that both towers were being treated the same but without repeating 'the two towers'. Because the author had previously used 'these' to refer to the foundations, he's had to be more specific and use the word 'tower' to ensure that the pronouns don't become confusing.
- ***masonry towers*** – by using 'masonry' to add detail to 'towers', the author tells the reader about the material from which the towers were built and so adds further information about the towers.

Resource sheet: Building the towers

Text 1

The bridge's deck hangs from cables that pass over the top of the two towers. The two towers stand in the river and were built with deep foundations. Digging the foundations for the two towers was a difficult and dangerous job. A huge box called a caisson was lowered to the river bed where the two towers were to stand. Builders climbed down into a chamber at the bottom of each caisson and dug out the mud and rock. The caissons were then filled with concrete and the two towers were built above them.

Text 2

The bridge's deck hangs from cables that pass over the top of the two towers. These towers, which stand in the river, were built with deep foundations. Digging these was a difficult and dangerous job. A huge box called a caisson was lowered to the river bed where each tower was to stand. Builders climbed down into a chamber at the bottom of each caisson and dug out the mud and rock. Then the caissons were filled with concrete and the masonry towers were built above them.

Grammar in action: writing an explanation text about a fantasy bridge — 1 session

Tell pupils that they are going to practise using the passive voice and cohesive devices such as pronouns while writing their own explanation about the construction of a bridge.

Ask them to draw a fantasy bridge design. They should label the construction techniques and components of their bridge using information from the extract to help them.

Give pupils a copy of the resource sheet *The Sky Bridge*. Discuss the use of passive voice and cohesive devices modelled in this example to help pupils recognise when and how to use them in their own writing.

Pupils should now use their design and the model text on the resource sheet to produce a written explanation about the construction of their fantasy bridge using the passive voice and cohesive devices.

Resource sheet: *The Sky Bridge*

The Sky Bridge is the world's first example of a floating bridge. This arched bridge was modelled on the Sydney Harbour Bridge but with significant modifications, which allow the bridge to float on air.

Each half of the Sky Bridge's huge arch was built out from a cloud toward its middle. Until the two halves were joined in the middle, huge water-crystal weights were fastened underneath each end. Fastening these weights was a dangerous job. Specialist engineers were flown up to the clouds by helicopter to attach them. Once the weights were secure, the roadway was added and the huge rainbow pylons were built at each end. The pylons hold the ends of the arch in place, meaning that the water-crystal weights are no longer needed.

Most of the water used in the construction of the Sky Bridge was sourced by squeezing rain clouds and freezing the water into super-strength icicles. These icicles were used to fasten the sections of the bridge in a similar manner to cables on a conventional bridge. Working on the Sky Bridge was cold work. Consequently, engineers were required to wear protective clothing to prevent frostbite.

The use of 'This' immediately after 'floating bridge' creates cohesion between this and the preceding sentence.

The use of the relative pronoun 'which' creates a relative clause adding further information about the bridge.

Most examples of the passive voice in this text do not refer to the person or 'agent' performing the action, which is a common feature of explanatory texts. The use of 'by' in this sentence makes the 'agent' or person performing the action clear.

The use of 'These icicles' immediately after 'super-strength icicles' creates cohesion between this and the preceding sentence.

Passive structures are used throughout the text. This focuses the reader on the processes being described rather than the people undertaking the actions.

The use of the noun phrase 'these weights' closely following 'water-crystal weights' binds the two sentences together, signalling that the second sentence is going to add further information about the weights.

The passive voice is used to ensure the focus in on the process rather than the person or agent bringing about the action.

Learning outcome: to use the subjunctive form to write a free verse poem

Keywords: stanzas, rhyming couplets, syllables, free verse, uncertainty, aspirations, modal verbs, subjunctive

WISH POEMS

If I Were King

I often wish I were a King,
And then I could do anything.

If only I were King of Spain,
I'd take my hat off in the rain.

If only I were King of France,
I wouldn't brush my hair for aunts.

I think, if I were King of Greece,
I'd push things off the mantelpiece.

If I were King of Norroway,
I'd ask an elephant to stay.

If I were King of Babylon,
I'd leave my button gloves undone.

If I were King of Timbuctoo,
I'd think of lovely things to do.

If I were King of anything,
I'd tell the soldiers, "I'm the King!"

By A. A. Milne

If I Were In Charge Of Our Park

If I were in charge of our park,
I'd remove all of the 'DO NOT WALK ON THE GRASS' signs,
All the 'NO BALL GAMES ALLOWED' signs,
And would replace them with an enormous
'PLEASE CLIMB THE TREES' notice.

If I were in charge of our park,
There would be a super-size swing,
And the world's slippiest slide.

If I were in charge of our park,
I would insist that parents were kept on leads,
That dogs were made to clean up their own mess
And that you could buy never-ending ice-cream.

If only I were in charge of our park.

By Rachel Clarke

Links to the National Curriculum

Reading – comprehension

- discuss and evaluate how authors use language, including figurative language, considering the impact on the reader

Writing – composition

- draft and write by selecting appropriate grammar and vocabulary, understanding how such choices can change and enhance meaning
- evaluate and edit by proposing changes to vocabulary, grammar and punctuation to enhance effects and clarify meaning
- perform their own compositions, using appropriate intonation, volume, and movement so that meaning is clear

Writing – vocabulary, grammar and punctuation

- recognise vocabulary and structures that are appropriate for formal speech and writing, including subjunctive forms
- use modal verbs or adverbs to indicate degrees of possibility

Reading the texts

1 session

Reading for meaning

Provide copies of the poems and read them aloud with pupils. Ask them to identify the theme of the poems (wishes). They should then reread the poems, annotating their copies to indicate the literary and poetic devices used by the poets (e.g. rhyming couplets, syllable patterns, figurative language).

Discuss the pupils' responses, making sure they have recognised the use of rhyming couplets and a regular syllable pattern in *'If I Were King'* compared with the free-verse characteristics of *'If I Were In Charge of Our Park'*. Ask them to identify how the rigid structure of *'If I Were King'* influenced the poet's word choices (e.g. rhyming 'France' with 'aunts' to maintain the rhyming pattern, writing 'Norroway' rather than 'Norway' to maintain the syllable pattern). Draw pupils' attention to the use of alliteration in *'If I Were In Charge of Our Park'* (super-size swing; the world's slippiest slide).

Reading for grammar

Tell pupils that they will be learning about some of the grammatical choices made by the poets so that they can write their own poem about wishes. Display the following sentences, asking pupils to identify which is correct and to explain their reasons:

I was reading a book.

I were reading a book.

Listen to their responses, clarifying that the first sentence is correct because the singular subject 'I' is being used with the singular past tense verb 'was'. In the second sentence, the singular subject 'I' and the plural verb 'were' do not agree.

Ask pupils to return to the poems and highlight the form of the verb 'to be' used by the poets. Pupils should notice that both poets have used 'were' even though they are writing in the singular.

Introduce the term 'subjunctive form', explaining that this is a verb form created by using 'were' to represent the verb 'to be'. Explain that the subjunctive is not used as frequently in everyday conversation as it once was, but that it is sometimes preferable when writing. Tell pupils that one use for the subjunctive form is to express wishes, dreams and aspirations.

Ask pupils to discuss whether wishes, dreams and aspirations are certain or uncertain. Listen to their responses, clarifying that wishes, dreams and aspirations are uncertain because they depend on other factors to be fulfilled. Ask pupils to look at the poems and identify a word used by both poets that indicates uncertainty (if). Explain that when we use 'if' to talk about something that is uncertain, we should use the 'were' form of the verb 'to be': the subjunctive.

Display the following sentences, asking pupils to indicate which shows the subjunctive (the second example).

If I was you, I'd go to the park.

I would join the scouts, if I were able.

Finally, ask pupils to note the modal verbs used in the poems (would, I'd, could). Explain that modal verbs are often used alongside 'if' when forming the subjunctive to express wishes, dreams and aspirations because they express uncertainty.

Independent task

Ask pupils to recall the poetic features of *'If I Were King'* (eight sets of rhyming couplets, eight syllables per line). Explain that they are going to use the subjunctive to write their own rhyming couplets in the style of the poem.

As a group, make a list of countries and words that rhyme with them (e.g. Britain / kitten, China / minor, Iraq / mac, India / windier, USA / hooray).

Model writing couplets, checking with pupils that each pair rhymes and that each line contains eight syllables. For example:

> If I were Queen of Great Britain,
> I'd have a tiny grey kitten.
> If I were ruler of Iraq,
> I wouldn't need to wear a mac.

When pupils have completed their couplets, they should underline their use of 'if' and 'were' and the modal verbs.

Support task

Distribute the resource sheet *Subjunctive sentences*. Read through the first three sentences together and ask pupils to discuss which are correct and which are incorrect. Listen to their responses, correcting them where necessary. Ask pupils to complete the rest of the sheet independently, ensuring that they understand how to complete each part. Early finishers should devise their own sentences using the subjunctive form.

Resource sheet: Subjunctive sentences

Read these sentences and discuss which use the subjunctive form.

1. I would give you extra pocket money if I was your mum.
2. If I were to win the lottery, I would take you on holiday.
3. I would be upset if I were told off by my teacher.

Complete these sentences so that they are written using the subjunctive form.

1. If I ________________ you, I would finish my homework as soon as possible.
2. She acts as if she ________________ the Queen of England.
3. Sam would make a great School Captain if he ________________ elected.
4. Humans may be able to fly, if they ________________ to grow wings.
5. If I ________________ a dog, I would enjoy chasing cats.

Tick to show which sentences use the subjunctive form.

1. James and Raj were playing in the park. ☐
2. If Sophie were in the orchestra, we would be much better. ☐
3. Zara and Mina were in Mrs Black's class. ☐
4. If I were a space explorer, I'd fly to the moon. ☐
5. If it were the last day of term, we'd have had an extra playtime today. ☐

Extension task

Ask pupils to reread the first stanza of *'If I Were King'*. Point out that it uses the subjunctive form, but 'if' has not been used. Remind them that the subjunctive is used when talking about wishes, dreams and aspirations. With this in mind, ask which word in the first sentence of *'If I Were King'* provides a clue that the subjunctive form needs to be used. Explain that the subjunctive has been formed using 'wish' and 'were'. Display the following examples to illustrate this further.

Sarah has gone to London. There are lots of landmarks there. I wish I were Sarah.

Ushma's dad has made vegetable soup for dinner. Ushma wishes she weren't having it.

Ask pupils to create some scenarios of their own using 'wish' and the subjunctive and to write these in their workbooks.

Evaluating and improving writing — 1 session

Provide pupils with the resource sheet *Cinderella*. Ask them to work in pairs to explore the conventions of play scripts that have been used and to consider how the script could be improved (e.g. remove inverted commas; add summary information to Scene 2; add information to explain why Cinderella shouts 'OUCH!').

Establish that the subjunctive form has not always been used appropriately. Ask pupils to circle the incorrect uses ('If I was lucky enough …'; 'I've always wished I was allowed').

Display an enlarged version of the play script. Work through the text with pupils, discussing their suggested changes and annotating the original text.

Ask pupils to write additional scenes, ensuring they use play script conventions and write in the subjunctive form when expressing wishes, dreams and aspirations.

Resource sheet: Cinderella

SCENE 1: THE BEDROOM *Cinderella is tidying up her older sisters' bedroom while they watch and think of more jobs for her to do.*

Ugly Sister 1: Cinderella, pick up my shoes and put away my clothes.

Ugly Sister 2: "Yes, and when you've done that you need to make my bed and clear away my empty cups," she said.

Cinderella: *(To herself)* If I was lucky enough to have my own room I wouldn't let it get this messy.

Ugly Sister 2: Ha. Well if we were more lucky we wouldn't have to look at you moping around feeling sorry for yourself all day long. Get downstairs and make our dinner.

SCENE 2: THE INVITATION ARRIVES

Messenger: (*Knocking on the door*) Message from the Prince for the ladies of the house.

(*Sound of three pairs of feet running down the hallway*)

Cinderella: Hello there, please come … OUCH!

Ugly Sister 1: If you were more considerate, you'd keep out of the way when we have important visitors.

Ugly Sister 2: (*Snatches letter and reads it to herself*) Cinderella, iron our ball gowns, find our best earrings and get the coach and horses ready. We're going to a ball.

Cinderella: I've always wished I was allowed to go to a ball.

Ugly Sister 1: Well you can wish all you like. If you were to come to the ball, everyone would stare at us. They'd wonder why we'd brought a scruffy servant with us.

Grammar in action: writing a poem about a wish or aspiration

1 session

Explain to pupils that they are going to write free verse poetry about wishes. Ask them to work in pairs to think of things they might wish for, such as being in charge of the school or being a space explorer, and what they would do with those wishes. Listen to their ideas and then model how to write a free verse poem using the resource sheet *Wish poem*. Talk about how the subjunctive is formed and how variety and interest have been created in the poem by placing the 'if' clause in different positions in the stanzas.

Discuss the clause order in the second line of the first stanza, noting that placing the 'if' clause first enables the list of wishes to flow more easily than if this clause came second.

Draw pupils' attention to the use of the modal verb 'would' throughout the poem. Ask them to consider if there are any other modals that may work in the poem (e.g. could).

Look at the use of 'allow' in the final stanza. Ask pupils to reflect on whether they think 'allow' or 'let' might work better here. Listen to their responses, suggesting that 'let' sounds less authoritative and as the poem is about being in charge, 'allow' sounds better.

When pupils have completed their poems, encourage them to read them to the rest of the class.

Resource sheet: Wish poem

I wish I were in charge of the school.
If I were granted this wish, I would cancel homework,
Detentions,
Extra maths lessons and running laps of the field in the rain.

I wouldn't ban the latest craze or game from the playground,
If I were in charge of the school.
I would use my wish to encourage children to bring in toys,
Swap comics
And play football.

If I were in charge of the school,
I would allow children to bring in sweets to share.
I would organise trips every week
And I would make playtime longer.

Oh, I wish I were in charge of the school.

The subjunctive formed with 'wish' and 'were'.

Model writing the clauses in this sentence the other way around, reflecting that placing the wish clause first enables the following list of wishes to flow more easily.

Draw attention to the use of the contraction. Reflect on how it helps create an informal tone in the poem.

The subjunctive formed with 'If' and 'were'.

Vocabulary choices reflect the aspiration of being in charge of the school.

The use of the exclamative 'Oh' adds emotion to the wish being expressed.

The subjunctive formed with 'wish' and 'were'.

UNIT 4: Recognising vocabulary and structures that are appropriate for formal speech and writing, including subjunctive forms

Learning outcome: to use the subjunctive form to write a formal letter containing school rules

Keywords: subjunctive, infinitive, colloquialism, informality, contractions, parenthesis, prefixes

Astro Academy

PROVIDING A GALACTIC-CLASS EDUCATION

www.astroacademy.cosmos   Contact: Headteacher@astroacademy.supernet.cosmos

Dear parents,

Welcome to Astro Academy. As you know, Astro Academy is the Galaxy's leading educational establishment and gaining a place is an immense privilege. We feel honoured to have such talented pupils in our school and therefore thank you for accepting a place at Astro Academy for your child.

At Astro Academy we recognise that education is a partnership between the school, parents and pupils. Therefore, we endeavour to provide your child with opportunities to fulfil their potential and become a truly galactic-class student. In return we ask that you support us by ensuring the following:

- that your child arrive punctually for school
- that you provide a quiet place for the completion of homework
- that you inform us of any absence from school at the earliest opportunity.

Standards of presentation are regarded highly at Astro Academy and we ask that all pupils be encouraged to comply with the uniform requirements by wearing the following:

- silver solar-energy jumpsuits
- black kinetic boots
- silver space helmets with reflective visors.

Further information about the school uniform can be found on the school website and items of uniform are available to purchase at the school shop.

We ask that you encourage your child to join the Pupil Voluntary Association. In the past, the association has raised funds to send its members on exchange trips to our partner school, Cosmos College; on orbital excursions around Saturn; and on history field trips to the site of the 20th-century moon landings.

We will be holding Pupil Consultation Evenings later this term where you can discuss how your child has settled into life at Astro Academy. Details of these meetings will be forwarded by your child's teacher in due course. In the meantime, if you have any concerns about your child's first days at Astro Academy, please do not hesitate to contact me.

Yours sincerely,

Xanti Lightspeed

Doctor Xanti Lightspeed

Message | Options

To: SamHalliday@email.co.uk

From: BenBrown@supermail.com

Subject: GOOD NEWS!!!!

Hi Sam,

How are things with you? I can't believe it – I've got a place at Astro Academy! This cool lady called Doctor Lightspeed came into school a few weeks back and asked to meet all the really hard-working kids. You should've seen her – blue skin, black hair – looked like she'd come straight out of a comic book.

Anyway, she gave all us hard workers a few questions to answer. Most of the other kids found them really tough, but they were all about the planets, aliens and space travel (you know how much I like that stuff). When we'd finished, she sent the other kids back to class and told me I'd got a place at Astro Academy. Cool, isn't it?

It sounds A-MAZ-ING! They have this cool uniform – it turns solar energy into electrical energy so you can power up your writing tablet and laser pen for the whole day. I know, LASER PEN! Cool, hey?

So that's it. I'm going. Mum and Dad thought nobody in our family would ever go to Astro Academy. But I am. Must've been all those space comics they kept telling me to put down!

See you soon,

Ben

Links to the National Curriculum

Reading – comprehension

- discuss and evaluate how authors use language, including figurative language, considering the impact on the reader

Writing – composition

- draft and write by selecting appropriate grammar and vocabulary, understanding how such choices can change and enhance meaning
- evaluate and edit by proposing changes to vocabulary, grammar and punctuation to enhance effects and clarify meaning

Writing – vocabulary, grammar and punctuation

- recognise vocabulary and structures that are appropriate for formal speech and writing, including subjunctive forms

TEACHING AND LEARNING IDEAS

Reading the texts

1 session

Reading for meaning

Distribute copies of the texts and read them aloud with pupils. Ask them to identify the purpose and audience of each (a letter of welcome addressed to parents; an email to a friend). Ask pupils where they think Astro Academy might be located (in space) and how the use of 'Astro' in the school's name might point to this ('astro-' is a prefix that refers to things associated with the stars and space). Ask pupils to locate other words and phrases in the letter that support the view that the school is located in space (e.g. 'galactic-class education'; www.astroacademy.cosmos; 'the Galaxy's leading educational establishment'; references to space helmets and trips to Saturn and the site of the moon landings). Explain that by using a variety of words and phrases associated with space, cohesion is created across the letter.

Reading for grammar

Ask pupils to identify, highlight and annotate the features in the letter and the email that demonstrate formality and informality. Discuss their responses, making sure they have identified features in the letter, such as: formal phrases ('purchase' rather than 'buy') and formal adverbials ('therefore'), and a general greeting ('Dear parents') rather than a personal greeting ('Hi Sam'). Compare these with the informal features in the email, such as: contractions ('I've'); question tags ('Cool, isn't it?'); capitals ('LASER PEN'); and dashes for parenthesis (' – blue skin, black hair – ').

Getting to grips with grammar

1 session

Independent task

Discuss what was learnt about the subjunctive in Unit 3. Explain that the subjunctive is also used to indicate the importance of something, such as an order, instruction or suggestion. This form of the subjunctive can be found in formal texts such as the letter in the extract. Display the following text with the verbs underlined as shown.

In return we ask that you <u>support</u> us by ensuring the following:

- that your child <u>arrive</u> punctually for school
- that you <u>provide</u> a quiet place for the completion of homework
- that you <u>inform</u> us of any absence from school at the earliest opportunity.

Draw pupils' attention to 'support', 'arrive', 'provide' and 'inform', noting that they are in the infinitive. Remind pupils that the infinitive is the simple form of a verb with 'to' (e.g. 'to go', 'to walk'). When forming the subjunctive, verbs should be in the infinitive but without the 'to' (e.g. 'go', 'walk').

Draw pupils' attention to the use of 'that' at the start of each request, explaining how it is used to help create this formal and directive form of the subjunctive. Ask pupils to identify the words giving the directive in this section of the text ('ask'; 'ensuring'). Explain that verbs such as 'ask' and 'ensure' are used with the subjunctive to indicate that something should be done.

Distribute the resource sheet *Writing in the subjunctive*. Ask pupils to read the sentences and to rewrite them using the subjunctive.

Resource sheet: Writing in the subjunctive

1. It is essential that your child arrives for school on time.
2. The headteacher suggested that Ravi played the guitar in assembly.
3. Dad demanded that Sophie cleans her bedroom.
4. It is imperative that Sam Halliday comes to school in his silver solar-energy jumpsuit.
5. "I insist that he stays inside until he finishes his work," said the strict teacher.

Early finishers should write their own subjunctive sentences using the verbs 'to drink', 'to talk' and 'to prepare'.

Support task

Talk to pupils about the subjunctive, explaining that when used to express orders, instructions or suggestions it uses the infinitive form of verbs but without the 'to'. Ask pupils to complete the resource sheet *The subjunctive.*

Resource sheet: The subjunctive

Write each of these infinitive verbs in the subjunctive.

infinitive	subjunctive
to advise	advise
to sing	
to ask	
to go	
to complete	

Complete the following sentences using the subjunctive verbs from the table and adding another clause.

e.g. We ask that you advise your child to wear a coat during the winter. (to advise)

1. Mrs Smith suggested that Sarah .... (to sing)
2. Mum insisted that I .... (to ask)
3. Auntie Steph suggested that we .... (to go)
4. I advise that you .... (to complete)

Extension task

Ask pupils to recall the different forms of the verb 'to be' (am, are, is, was, were, be, being, been). Explain that as the verb 'to be' is used frequently in English, 'be' is often used to form the subjunctive. Distribute copies of the resource sheet *Practising using the subjunctive*. Ask pupils to read the first three sentences and to identify the subjunctive in each. Then ask them to rewrite the rest of the sentences so that each one uses the subjunctive.

Resource sheet: Practising using the subjunctive

Identify the subjunctive in each of these sentences:

1. We ask that all pupils be encouraged to comply with the uniform requirements.
2. Is it essential that we be there?
3. I asked that Joe not be at my birthday party.

Now rewrite these sentences using the subjunctive:

1. Mr Fry says it is crucial that you are at the coach station 30 minutes before departure time.
2. It is essential that all members of the school council are at the next meeting.
3. It is imperative that your writing is as neat as possible.
4. It is essential that children are able to recite their times tables.
5. I suggest that the football match is rearranged if it rains.
6. Mr Smith said it was vital that our homework was completed promptly.
7. Mum said, 'It is essential that you are waiting for Dad when he comes to collect you.'
8. Anna suggested that Tim and I were asked to join the chess club.

Evaluating and improving writing 1 session

Talk about the degree of formality required for letters of application. Provide pupils with the resource sheet *Sam's letter* and ask them to think about how the formality could be increased.

Display an enlarged version of the letter. Work through the text with pupils, discussing their suggestions and annotating the original. Changes could include: amending the salutation to 'Dear Dr Lightspeed'; removing the question tag; and removing colloquialisms such as 'snappy dresser'.

Ask pupils to rewrite the letter using the subjunctive to increase the formality (e.g. 'I am writing to ask that you consider me for a place at Astro Academy.').

Resource sheet: Sam's letter

5 Light Lane
Townley
Smallshire

Hi there Dr Lightspeed,

Sam here. You know my friend Ben, don't you? He just got a place at Astro Academy and now I've heard how cool it is, I want to come too. I work really hard and always try my best. I'm a bit of a snappy dresser so wearing solar-energy jumpsuits and kinetic boots sounds really cool. I think the trips sound brilliant too. I've always fancied seeing the rings of Saturn.

I think I'd be a pretty useful member of the Pupil Voluntary Association as I'm on the school council at my current school. I help with all the events – you should've seen my dancing at the last disco!

I think I'd make a fantastic Astro Academy pupil. Please let me come.

Best wishes,

Sam Halliday

Grammar in action: writing a formal letter using the subjunctive 1 session

Tell pupils they are going to use the subjunctive to write a formal letter asking parents to ensure that the school rules are kept. Use the resource sheet *The school rules* to model writing the letter. Highlight the use of:

- formal phrases such as 'come to our attention' instead of 'we have noticed'
- the infinitive 'wear' and 'provide' to form the subjunctive
- the subjunctive of the verb 'to be' in 'that children <u>be</u> healthy' and 'that treats <u>be</u> included' rather than 'that children are healthy' and 'that treats are included'
- bullet points to ensure the directives stand out from the rest of the text.

After modelling, ask pupils to think about rules they would like to implement and to practise phrasing these using the subjunctive. They should then write their own letters using a formal style and including their rules.

Resource sheet: The school rules

Casual College
Townley
Smallshire

Dear Parents,

It has come to our attention that several pupils are failing to maintain the school's high standards. We ask that you discuss this issue with your child as a matter of urgency and support us by considering the following points:

- In order to ensure comfort, we ask that all pupils wear trainers or sports shoes.
- It is imperative that all pupils feel relaxed in lessons. To ensure this, we ask that parents provide pupils with tracksuits, joggers and sweatshirts.
- Pupils have expressed concern that parents routinely pack healthy lunches. Whilst we appreciate parental concern that children be healthy, we ask that snacks and treats be included in all lunchboxes.

We thank you for your support in this matter and ask that any questions or queries about this issue be directed to the school office.

Yours sincerely,

Mrs R Ward

Headteacher

Learning outcome: to write an information text explaining how to build a den

Keywords: organisational devices, consistent, colon, consistency

THE STICK BOOK: LOADS OF THINGS YOU CAN MAKE OR DO WITH A STICK

Discovering sticks

Let's go on an adventure. All you have to do is run outside and find a stick. Choose it with care and it can be anything you want it to be: a sword with which to fight off fierce dragons in the forest, a tracking stick to help you creep after secretive creatures, a wand to cast magic spells or a broomstick to transport you to other worlds.

The stick is perhaps the best-loved toy of all time, the starting point for endless adventures for generations of children all over the world. Sticks are easy to find, natural and, best of all, totally free. So, if you haven't got your own special stick, what are you waiting for?

The Stick Book is packed with activities to do with big sticks and little sticks, with dead sticks gathered from the ground and green sticks cut from living trees. Sticks are part of the natural world, providing food and shelter for birds and animals, so always collect them with care. In particular, cut green sticks very carefully so as not to damage trees.

While you can do a lot with sticks on their own, you can do even more by adding a few other simple materials.

Clay: Wild clay can be collected from the banks of clean ditches and streams. (Alternatively, you can buy clay from educational suppliers or good toy shops.)

Natural paints: To make natural paints you need a pestle and mortar and some water.
Try making white paint from crushed chalk, brown or grey paint from clay mixed with water, black paint from crushed charcoals and red and purple paint from strained berries.

Stick adventure bag: If you want to make the most of every trip outdoors, prepare a stick adventure bag, packed with:

- String, raffia, wool, thin wire and elastic bands
- Masking tape, double-sided sticky tape, PVA glue
- Old paintbrushes and sponges
- Scissors, secateurs and a sharp bushcraft knife, and small torches or night lights in jars (only include these if you are accompanied by a grown-up)
- A basic first aid kit

Wherever you are and whatever the weather, we hope ***The Stick Book*** will inspire you to get outdoors and discover the wonders of sticks and some of the secrets of the natural world.

Share the magic of a fire

NEVER make a fire without grown-ups present.

- It's usually best to make your fire in a metal pan (a dustbin lid, hubcap or old wok), to keep it confined. Put the pan on rocks, wood or metal legs to avoid scorching the ground. If you make a fire on the ground, clear away leaf litter or cut out turf to give a base of bare soil.
- Collect tinder (dry fine material such as dried bracken or fluffy seed) along with dead, dry twigs and sticks; this helps to get the fire going. Make a tepee of twigs as described below.
- The kindling tepee will eventually collapse. Let it form a hot bed of embers for cooking on or build it up again for warmth.
- Let the fire burn out. When it's completely cold, cover or remove the ash. Leave the site exactly as you found it.

Build a tepee of little twigs (kindling) over a bundle of tinder. Strike a match as close to the tinder as possible. When the tinder starts burning, add twigs, and then larger sticks as the fire builds.

The Stick Book: Loads of things you can make or do with a stick by Fiona Danks and Jo Schofield

Links to the National Curriculum

Reading – comprehension

- maintain positive attitudes to reading and understanding of what they read by continuing to read and discuss an increasingly wide range of fiction, poetry, plays, non-fiction and reference books or textbooks
- understand what they read by identifying how language, structure and presentation contribute to meaning

Writing – composition

- draft and write by using further organisational and presentational devices to structure text and to guide the reader [for example, headings, bullet points, underlining]
- draft and write by précising longer passages

Writing – vocabulary, grammar and punctuation

- indicate grammatical and other features by punctuating bullet points consistently

TEACHING AND LEARNING IDEAS

Reading the text

1 session

Reading for meaning

Distribute copies of the extract and read it with pupils, asking them to identify its purpose (to give information about things to do with sticks) and audience (children). Ask them to identify and highlight the organisational features, annotating their copies to indicate the effectiveness of each feature (e.g. The subheading 'Discovering sticks' tells readers what the section is about; the italics indicate that *The Stick Book* is the name of the book they are reading; parenthetical brackets indicate additional information). Listen to their responses, clarifying where appropriate.

Ask pupils to identify the purpose of the text box at the end of the extract. Explain how it clarifies the meaning of 'a tepee of twigs', making this key information more prominent than if it had been included in the body of the text.

Reading for grammar

Ask pupils to identify which section gives information about the equipment that is required when playing with sticks ('*Stick adventure bag*'). Ask what they notice about the organisation of the information in this section (bullet points). Explain that bullet points are organisational devices that present information clearly and concisely. Display the sentence 'The greengrocer sells the following: apples, bananas, carrots and potatoes' and show pupils how to present it with bullet points:

The greengrocer sells the following:

- apples
- bananas
- carrots
- potatoes.

Explain that the list is introduced with a colon and that each item sits on its own bullet-pointed line and begins with a lowercase letter. Explain that whilst there are no firm grammatical rules about punctuating bullet points, it is important that writers are consistent in their use of capitals, commas and semi-colons across a piece of writing.

Display the sentence 'To help keep our school tidy, please: put your rubbish in the bin; hang coats on the pegs in the cloakroom; and put all equipment away after using it.' Ask pupils to rewrite it with bullet points:

To help keep our school tidy, please:

- put your rubbish in the bin
- hang coats on the pegs in the cloakroom
- put all equipment away after using it.

Explain that semi-colons could be used at the end of each line, but they are not necessary; the bullet points are separating each part of the list already.

Ask pupils what they notice about the bullet points used in the section '*Share the magic of a fire*'. They should note that each bullet point is a stage in the construction of a fire and that full sentences have been used because the bullets are full sentences. In this instance, a colon has not been used to introduce the bullets as they are not an extension of a sentence.

Independent task

Distribute copies of the resource sheet *Creating bulleted lists* and ask pupils to rewrite each sentence using bullet points.

Resource sheet: Creating bulleted lists

1. For lunch today I had a sandwich, some crisps, a yoghurt and a carton of orange drink.
2. Our rugby players wear black shirts, black shorts, and black and gold socks.
3. When you make pancakes you need eggs, flour, milk, a pinch of salt and a frying pan.
4. Children need to bring the following on the school trip: a swimming costume; sturdy walking boots; a waterproof coat; warm trousers and tops.
5. At the safari park you can see herds of buffalo; families of monkeys; prides of lions; and groups of tourists taking photographs.

When they have finished, check pupils' work for accuracy. Encourage early finishers to write some of their own lists punctuated with bullet points.

Support task

Distribute the resource sheet *Bullet points*. Ask pupils to cut out the sentence starters and items, arrange them as a bulleted list and then write the sentences out using bullets and consistent punctuation and capitalisation.

Resource sheet: Bullet points

Sasha made a fruit salad using	bananas	apples	grapes	strawberries	pears
We've got these things in our shed	a spade	two footballs	a lawnmower	an old pair of wellies	
Dogs like	going for walks	chewing bones	chasing sticks	lots and lots of cuddles	
On her desk, Mrs Brown has	a stapler	a pile of unmarked books	a pot of pens and pencils	a stopwatch	a large packet of sweets

Extension task

Ask pupils to list the characters in Hansel and Gretel (a father, a stepmother, two children called Hansel and Gretel, and a witch). Explain that you are going to write a series of PowerPoint slides about Hansel and Gretel, starting with this information. For example:

Characters in Hansel and Gretel

The following characters appear in Hansel and Gretel:

- *the children's father*
- *heir stepmother*
- *Hansel*
- *Gretel*
- *the witch*

With pupils, discuss the various settings used in the story of Hansel and Gretel (their home, the forest, the witch's house) and write this as a bulleted PowerPoint slide. Then create a slide summarising the main points of the plot (the children leave home, they make their way through the forest with breadcrumbs, they stumble across the witch's house and eat parts of it, they are taken captive, their father comes and rescues them).

Ask pupils to recall other well-known traditional tales and to make a series of PowerPoint slides outlining the characters, setting and plot summary. When they have made their PowerPoint slides, they should check them for accuracy and consistency.

Evaluating and improving writing — 1 session

Ask pupils to proofread and edit the resource sheet *Huge elephant fact file*. They should:

- make sure all the bullet points are punctuated consistently
- consider the consistency of layout techniques such as headings and subheadings
- consider the use of abbreviations such as kg/kilogram and l/litre
- make sure sections are introduced consistently.

When they have finished, discuss pupils' work and ask them to explain their choices.

Resource sheet: Huge elephant fact file

Huge elephant fact file	
TWO TYPES OF ELEPHANT • There are two types of elephants; Asian Elephants and African Elephants • wild elephants live in Asia and Africa. • African elephants are larger than Asian elephants and have larger ears • the Asian elephant has one finger on the end of the trunk the African has two.	**Trunk facts** Probably the most iconic feature of the elephant is its trunk. The trunk is used for; ♦ Drinking; ♦ Smelling ♦ Breathing ♦ picking up food ♦ Touching; ♦ communicating Elephants love squirting themselves with water using their trunk like a shower.
How big are elephants Elephants are the largest land mammals in the world ♦ Elephants weigh around 90 kilograms when they are born. ♦ adult elephants weigh between 2 tons and 7 tons; ♦ the height of elephants is between 2.5 and 4 metres	**<u>Have you ever wondered what elephants eat?</u>** Elephants are herbivores; they don't eat meat. In the wild elephants eat grass, leaves, shrubs, branches and fruit. Food facts; • They spend 16 hours a day eating. • Adult elephants eat 150–300 kg of food every day. • Elephants drink 180–225 litres of water every day.

Grammar in action: writing a bulleted text about building an indoor den — 1 session

Tell pupils they are going to use organisational features such as headings, subheadings, text boxes and bullet points when writing a text about building an indoor den. Prior to writing, pupils should research den-building techniques by entering 'how to build an indoor den' into an internet search engine. If possible, they should build their own den.

Model how to write the text, using the resource sheet *How to build an indoor den* to help you.

- Talk about the use of 'surveillance' in the title and how words such as 'prying' and 'secret hide-out' link to this and help to create cohesion.
- Discuss the use of bullet points to present the 'You will need' section and remind pupils of the importance of maintaining consistency.

- Talk about the 'Construction method' section, explaining that there are no adverbials of time or numbered bullets as some parts of the process could be done in a different order.
- Explain that the closing paragraph signals the end of the instructions and feels more complete than if the text finished after the final bullet point.

After working through the resource sheet, ask pupils to use the information from their earlier research to write their own information text. Remind them to include organisational features to ensure their information is clear and concise.

Resource sheet: How to build an indoor den

Building a sitting room surveillance den

Building a place free from the prying eyes of adults is great fun. All you need are some everyday items and a bit of creativity and you too can have a secret hide-out in your sitting room.

You will need

The basic requirements for a den are as follows:

- a warm, cosy space – adult-free if possible
- blankets, sheets and bedcovers – plenty of these
- furniture – any you can lay your hands on
- cushions – sofa cushions are best
- clothes pegs – the springy type work best.

Construction method

- Choose your construction site. Avoid areas that people frequently walk through; you don't want nosy neighbours walking past while you're holding top secret meetings.
- Select the furniture for the walls of your den. High-backed chairs are useful as they ensure plenty of headroom once you add the roof to your den.
- Locate the best blankets, sheets and bedcovers you can find. Bedcovers make great roofs; blankets are good for walls and floors.
- Fasten the bedcovers, sheets and blankets together with clothes pegs. Joining your roof and wall together means that passing spies are unable to see into your den.
- Make your den cosy and comfortable by dragging in the squishiest cushions you can find. Sofa cushions are great but you may find that your resident adults attempt to retrieve them.

Once built, use your den to plan secret missions, hold important meetings and eavesdrop on enemy conversations. Your den will last for as long as your mission requires or until your resident adult issues a land-clearance order.

Getting the most from your den

- Make a KEEP OUT! sign to show outsiders that the den is PRIVATE.
- Find a box (with a lock if possible) to keep notebooks and plans away from the eyes of enemy spies.
- Ensure your den is well stocked with tasty snacks. You don't want hunger pangs to distract you from your secret mission.
- Ensure there is a torch in your den. You need to keep a light on your secret plans.
- Invite your favourite teddies and stuffed toys to act as guards in your den. You can always snuggle up with them if they fall asleep on duty.

Learning outcome: to write a descriptive passage about an animal discovery

Keywords: coordinate, contrast, link, pause

FENN HALFLIN AND THE FEARZERO

At the end of the jetty he caught sight of the red-sailed barge, which had just moored. On its side, in peeling paint, he could just make out the name: The *Salamander*. Quiet as a cat, he slunk against the *Gloriana's* flank, keeping tight inside the fringe of her shadow.

The *Salamander* was unloved. Fishing nets lay strewn untidily on deck and the cabin windows were clogged with green mildew. There seemed to be a small crew; only three men in total, which was unusual for a fishing barge. Fenn guessed they were Scotians; they looked like some of Viktor's crew. Their bushy, red-gold hair was matted and their faces were sunburned to the colour of lobster. They had clearly sailed from warmer waters.

Fenn struggled to contain his excitement. It was a fishing ship; fishing and salvage, he guessed. It would probably have a big hold where they could all hide, so long as it wasn't already packed to the brim with cargo or so empty that they'd be seen immediately.

Fenn decided to slip aboard and check it out before alerting the others. He waited while the crew secured the barge, learning from their shouted calls that the ratty-looking one with the scrappy beard was Owen, and that the larger, sloping shouldered one was Logan. These two called the third man – who was the oldest – Captain; he was a burly man with a squashed face like he'd run hard into a wall. After a few minutes he left, passing within a whisker of Fenn who was crouching in the shadows. The captain disappeared straight up into the hole in the *Gloriana* – the *Salamander* had obviously landed here before. As soon as the others' backs were turned, Fenn scampered to the barge and slipped aboard. He was just about to run over to the hold when Logan suddenly loped back along the deck. Fenn had no choice but to dive down the stairs.

Inside, the *Salamander* was in a sorry state, but that was good news Fenn reckoned; a slovenly crew wouldn't be making inspections or be down in the hold setting rat traps every night. Fenn crept into a kitchen where he found a squalid mess; a pot of something sat on the stove with mould creeping over it, so thick and fluffy it looked like a pan of fur. Used plates had been dropped in a bucket of putrid water with food and dead maggots floating on the surface, and empty bottles of whisky lay broken on the floor. He waited a few moments to see which way Logan went, then suddenly heard his footsteps coming down the deck steps. Panicking, Fenn pushed open the next door and slipped behind it.

He found himself in a surprisingly neat little cabin, fitted out with small beds; basic, not the height of luxury, but better than anything he'd slept on in a long time. Judging from the size of the beds he realised this wasn't a fishing vessel at all; they weren't adult-sized. It looked like a convoy ship, similar to the one Fathom had talked about; shipping children to safety. Fenn wondered if any of the Shantie children would be lucky enough to get passage; recalling rumours that some were taken to foster parents behind the Walls. But if it was a convoy ship, why moor here, in secret? He listened as Logan thumped around in the kitchen for a bit, then he heard the sound of breaking glass, some swearing, and finally his footfall retreating back up the steps.

Suddenly his thoughts were interrupted by more voices directly above him; a woman's and a child's, then the sound of them getting closer. Fenn stumbled backwards in the dark and found himself against a cupboard door. He swiftly slid inside and shut it quietly behind him, just as the door to the cabin opened.

Fenn Halflin and the Fearzero by Francesca Armour-Chelu

Links to the National Curriculum

Reading – comprehension

- maintain positive attitudes to reading and understanding of what they read by increasing their familiarity with a wide range of books, including myths, legends and traditional stories, modern fiction, fiction from our literary heritage, and books from other cultures and traditions
- discuss and evaluate how authors use language, including figurative language, considering the impact on the reader

Writing – composition

- draft and write by, in narratives, describing settings, characters and atmosphere and integrating dialogue to convey character and advance the action

Writing – vocabulary, grammar and punctuation

- indicate grammatical and other features by using semi-colons, colons or dashes to mark boundaries between independent clauses

TEACHING AND LEARNING IDEAS

Reading the text

1 session

Reading for meaning

Distribute copies of the extract and read it aloud with pupils. Explain that the extract is from a story about a boy called Fenn who is on a quayside. He has just explored a moored ship called the *Gloriana* and is about to discover another mysterious ship: the *Salamander*. Ask pupils to reread the passage, highlighting information about the appearance of the *Salamander*. Discuss the information they have highlighted, drawing out descriptions such as: a barge with red sails; peeling paintwork; windows covered in mildew.

Reading for grammar

Explain to pupils that they are going to look at the author's use of semi-colons in this passage in order to learn how to use semi-colons when writing their own descriptive passage.

Tell pupils that semi-colons can be used in two ways: to separate lists of information in a similar way to commas; and to link separate but closely related clauses. Display the following examples:

- You can see lots of different vehicles at the motor museum: double-decker buses with spiral staircases; old motorbikes; glossy, old-fashioned bicycles; and polished, gleaming antique cars.
- The boy was racing down the street; a dog was chasing him.

Explain how the semi-colons in the list ease understanding by making the pause between each description stronger than if commas had been used. Draw pupils' attention to the colon at the beginning of the list, explaining how colons can introduce new ideas, which is why they are used to introduce lists.

Talk about the second example, explaining that the two clauses could have been written as separate sentences, or joined with a conjunction, for example:

- The boy was racing down the street. A dog was chasing him.
- The boy was racing down the street and a dog was chasing him.

Explain that coordinating the clauses with a semi-colon shows that they're closely related; the pause between the clauses is shorter than a full stop.

Ask pupils to reread the extract and highlight the semi-colons. They should decide whether each semi-colon separates items in a list or joins clauses of information. Discuss their ideas, confirming that all the semi-colons in the passage link clauses of information.

Getting to grips with grammar

1 session

Independent task

Display the following sentence and ask pupils to indicate whether the semi-colon separates items in a list or coordinates closely related clauses:

> The playground was deserted; there were no children to be seen anywhere.

Listen to their responses, clarifying that in this sentence the semi-colon joins two closely related clauses. Distribute copies of the resource sheet *Using semi-colons to write sentences*. Explain how to use the ideas from the Clause 1 column and the Clause 2 column of the table to write sentences containing two related clauses separated by a semi-colon. Pupils should be as creative as they can when writing their sentences (e.g. The door creaked open; a ghostly figure stepped in.).

Resource sheet: Using semi-colons to write sentences

Clause 1	Clause 2
The door opens	someone steps in
A noisy library	Class 5 paying a visit
Buying a new toy	playing with it straightaway
Rainy weather	flooded houses
Being tired	a sleepover
Being excited	something special is going to happen

Early finishers should write further sentences using their own ideas and semi-colons to coordinate closely related clauses.

Support task

Talk about how semi-colons can be used to join two closely related clauses. Explain that sometimes the clauses could have been joined with a conjunction or left as separate sentences marked with a full stop. By choosing to use semi-colons, we can show that the two clauses are closely related. Demonstrate by displaying the following:

The weather was windy. Leaves flew through the air.

The weather was windy and leaves flew through the air.

The weather was windy; leaves flew through the air.

Distribute copies of the resource sheet *Semi-colons*, explaining that pupils should add semi-colons in the correct places.

Resource sheet: Semi-colons

1. The children looked very smart in the photograph. Their uniforms were neat and tidy.
2. The stadium filled up quickly. Everyone was looking forward to the game.
3. The boat looked untidy and its nets lay in a tangled heap.
4. Anita was a great netball player and she scored lots of goals.
5. Nadia was hiding in the bushes and she was hoping nobody would find her.

Extension task

Talk to pupils about the roles performed by semi-colons: to separate items in a list and to join closely related clauses. Display the following scenarios and show pupils how to write a sentence about the scenario using semi-colons.

Scenario: Icy weather and slippery pavements.

Sentence: It had been icy all week; the pavements were as slippery as an ice rink.

Scenario: A detailed list about a busy zookeeper's job.

Sentence: The zookeeper was extremely busy as he had to: feed the giraffes; find the monkey's favourite toys; clean the lions' enclosure; fill the penguins' pond with water; and find the escaped tarantula.

Distribute the resource sheet *Scenarios and semi-colons.* Ask pupils to use semi-colons to write a sentence about each scenario:

Resource sheet: Scenarios and semi-colons

1. frightened children being followed by a ghost
2. feeling nervous and a school play
3. a detailed list of what you did at the weekend
4. a description of a scruffy-looking boat with peeling paint
5. a detailed list about a busy day at the seaside

When they have finished, they should write their own sentences demonstrating the different uses of semi-colons.

Evaluating and improving writing — 1 session

Provide pupils with copies of the resource sheet *The Salamander.* Read the two descriptive passages to pupils and then ask them to work in pairs to discuss what they like and dislike about each extract and how they think each could be improved. Discuss their thoughts, drawing out the following points:

- The over-use of semi-colons in Example 1 becomes repetitive. Example 2 would benefit from some semi-colons to show the close relationship between some of the sentences.
- Words have been chosen for effect in Example 2 (e.g. littered, peeled, drooped).
- Imagery is created through the use of personification in Example 2 (e.g. 'red sails drooped miserably', 'bowls and cutlery drowned in a bucket of greasy water').
- Cohesion is created in Example 2 through the use of words associated with neglect (e.g. disarray, neglected, long-ignored).

Pupils should rewrite and extend the passage by using the best parts from each example, choosing when to use semi-colons to coordinate clauses and to separate items in lists.

Resource sheet: *The Salamander*

Example 1

The *Salamander* was a fishing barge; its decks were covered in fishing nets making it look untidy. Paint peeled from its sides; mildew covered the windows; and the masts held up limp red sails. Inside the *Salamander* it was hard to see; there were no lights. In the kitchen, the smell of rotting food came from the dirty plates; cups, bowls and cutlery were in a bucket of water; maggots ate fish bones. The *Salamander* was an unloved ship; clearly not a home.

Example 2

The *Salamander* was a fishing barge. Fishing nets littered the deck, creating a sense of disarray. It was neglected and paint peeled from its hull. Mildew grew over the windows and its red sails drooped miserably from their masts. It was hard to see inside the *Salamander* because there were no lights. The stench of putrefying food wafted up from the kitchen. Filthy plates, cups, bowls and cutlery drowned in a bucket of greasy water and maggots feasted on long-ignored fish bones. The *Salamander* was an unloved vessel. It was clearly not a home.

Grammar in action: using semi-colons to write a narrative

1 session

Before the session, display a consequences-style drawing with a bear's head, a monkey's arms, a fish's body, a bear's legs and a rabbit's feet. Explain to pupils that they are going to write a descriptive passage using semi-colons to separate items in lists and to link related clauses.

Start by asking pupils if they have ever played consequences. Explain the game by showing them your drawing and then invite pairs or groups of pupils to take turns to draw parts of an animal, fold the paper over and pass it on.

Once pupils have created their animal pictures, use the resource sheet *Consequences creature* to model writing a descriptive passage about the creature in your drawing.

- Talk about how the opening of the account places the description in a place (the southern seas).
- Talk about how the name of the Scaled Monkey-Bear is introduced after a colon, to mirror the way the *Salamander* was introduced in the earlier text.
- Draw pupils' attention to the adverbial and the use of a semi-colon to coordinate clauses in the sentence 'Upon observing the creature, we saw it had a large head; it was furry and shaped ...'.
- Model making word choices and changing them to show the impact of interesting words. Start by writing 'green' instead of 'lush', 'body' instead of 'torso' and 'shiny' instead of 'iridescent'.

After modelling, ask pupils to use their consequences drawings to write their own animal descriptions using semi-colons.

Resource sheet: Consequences creature

We had been sailing across the southern seas for four months when we finally spotted land. Restless and desperate to press our feet into firm ground, we moored our vessel and headed into the lush rainforest ahead. Within minutes of entering the forest we made the discovery of a lifetime: the Scaled Monkey-Bear.

This legendary creature had featured in the stories of forest-dwellers; the songs and poems of travelling musicians; and the vivid imaginations of young children. But until our sighting, it had not been documented in detail.

Upon observing the creature, we saw it had a large head; it was furry and shaped like that of a grizzly bear. Unlike any bear we had seen before, its fur was blue and stood on end as if the creature had received an electric shock. Moving down to the creature's torso, we could see that it was covered in scales; these were not the iridescent scales of a fish but a matt, unreflective armour. The animal's arms were like those of a monkey; they were joined to its body at the neck rather than the shoulder. It had nimble fingers that it clicked continually as if marking the rhythm of a song.

Beneath the torso, the creature had the wide, powerful legs of a bear. However, instead of the wide paws of a bear, its feet were more like those of a rabbit.

Learning outcome: to write a persuasive text containing hyphens

Keywords: compound noun, compound adjective, ambiguity

THE WIND IN THE WILLOWS

There was the noise of a bolt shot back, and the door opened a few inches, enough to show a long snout and a pair of sleepy blinking eyes.

"Now, the *very* next time this happens," said a gruff and suspicious voice, "I shall be exceedingly angry. Who is it *this* time, disturbing people on such a night? Speak up!"

"O, Badger," cried the Rat, "let us in, please. It's me, Rat, and my friend Mole, and we've lost our way in the snow."

"What, Ratty, my dear little man!" exclaimed the Badger, in quite a different voice. "Come along in, both of you, at once. Why, you must be perished. Well I never! Lost in the snow! And in the Wild Wood too, and at this time of night! But come in with you."

The two animals tumbled over each other in their eagerness to get inside, and heard the door shut behind them with great joy and relief.

The Badger, who wore a long dressing-gown, and whose slippers were indeed very down-at-heel, carried a flat candlestick in his paw and had probably been on his way to bed when their summons sounded. He looked kindly down on them and patted both their heads. "This is not the sort of night for small animals to be out," he said paternally. "I'm afraid you've been up to some of your pranks again, Ratty. But come along; come into the kitchen. There's a first-rate fire there, and supper and everything."

He shuffled on in front of them, carrying the light, and they followed him, nudging each other in an anticipating sort of way, down a long, gloomy, and to tell the truth, decidedly shabby passage, into a sort of a central hall, out of which they could dimly see other long tunnel-like passages branching, passages mysterious and without apparent end. But there were doors in the hall as well – stout oaken comfortable-looking doors. One of these the Badger flung open, and at once they found themselves in all the glow and warmth of a large fire-lit kitchen.

The floor was well-worn red brick, and on the wide hearth burnt a fire of logs, between two attractive chimney-corners tucked away in the wall, well out of any suspicion of draught. A couple of high-backed settles, facing each other on either side of the fire, gave further sitting accommodation for the sociably disposed. In the middle of the room stood a long table of plain boards placed on trestles, with benches down each side. At one end of it, where an arm-chair stood pushed back, were spread the remains of the Badger's plain but ample supper. Rows of spotless plates winked from the shelves of the dresser at the far end of the room, and from the rafters overhead hung hams, bundles of dried herbs, nets of onions, and baskets of eggs.

It seemed a place where heroes could fitly feast after victory, where weary harvesters could line up in scores along the table and keep their Harvest Home with mirth and song, or where two or three friends of simple tastes could sit about as they pleased and eat and smoke and talk in comfort and contentment. The ruddy brick floor smiled up at the smoky ceiling; the oaken settles, shiny with long wear, exchanged cheerful glances with each other; plates on the dresser grinned at pots on the shelf, and the merry firelight flickered and played over everything without distinction.

The kindly Badger thrust them down on a settle to toast themselves at the fire, and bade them remove their wet coats and boots. Then he fetched them dressing-gowns and slippers, and himself bathed the Mole's shin with warm water and mended the cut with sticking-plaster till the whole thing was just as good as new, if not better. In the embracing light and warmth, warm and dry at last, with weary legs propped up in front of them, and a suggestive clink of plates being arranged on the table behind, it seemed to the storm-driven animals, now in safe anchorage, that the cold and trackless Wild Wood just left outside was miles and miles away, and all that they had suffered in it a half-forgotten dream.

The Wind in the Willows by Kenneth Grahame

Links to the National Curriculum

Reading – comprehension

- maintain positive attitudes to reading and understanding of what they read by increasing their familiarity with a wide range of books, including myths, legends and traditional stories, modern fiction, fiction from our literary heritage, and books from other cultures and traditions
- discuss and evaluate how authors use language, including figurative language, considering the impact on the reader

Writing – composition

- plan their writing by identifying the audience for and purpose of the writing, selecting the appropriate form and using other similar writing as models for their own
- proof-read for spelling and punctuation errors

Writing – vocabulary, grammar and punctuation

- indicate grammatical and other features by using hyphens to avoid ambiguity

TEACHING AND LEARNING IDEAS

Reading the text

1 session

Reading for meaning

Provide copies of the extract and read it aloud with pupils. Ask them to recount the events, the setting and the names of the characters. Ask pupils to reread the extract, identifying words they are unsure of. Talk about these words, providing definitions where necessary.

Ask pupils to discuss the extract, deciding whether it is modern or old and identifying features that support their opinion (e.g. it is old: words like *hearth*, *settles* and *dresser* are not used much now).

Ask pupils to locate examples of personification in the penultimate paragraph of the extract (e.g. 'The ruddy brick floor smiled …'; 'the oaken settles … exchanged cheerful glances …'). Encourage them to discuss the effectiveness of the technique (e.g. it creates an effect of friendliness as the objects are smiling and grinning at each other).

Reading for grammar

Tell pupils they will be looking at the author's use of hyphens in order to write their own persuasive text containing hyphens.

Explain that, in this extract, the author has used hyphens for two purposes. In the first instance, nouns have been joined with hyphens to make compound nouns (nouns made from more than one word). For example: 'The Badger, who wore a long <u>dressing-gown</u> …'

In the second instance, descriptive words have been joined with hyphens to make compound adjectives (adjectives made from more than one word). For example: 'There's a <u>first-rate</u> fire …'

Ask pupils to scan the text to locate hyphenated words. They should list these under the headings 'compound nouns' (dressing-gown; chimney-corners; arm-chair; sticking-plaster) and 'compound adjectives' (first-rate; tunnel-like; comfortable-looking; fire-lit; well-worn; high-backed; storm-driven; half-forgotten). Draw pupils' attention to 'down-at-heel', explaining that this is a compound adjective made from three words which means 'shabby'.

Explain how, over time, some compound nouns lose their hyphens. Armchair is now written as one word. That it is hyphenated in this extract, is an indication that this is an older text.

Getting to grips with grammar

1 session

Independent task

Display the following sentences:

My aunt is a short story writer.   My aunt is a short-story writer.

Ask pupils to discuss the sentences and explain the meaning of each. Clarify that the first sentence suggests the aunt is short in height and the second sentence indicates that she writes stories that are short. Discuss how 'short-story' describes the type of author the aunt is. Explain that when describing nouns, we should think carefully about whether the descriptive words need hyphenating to make our meaning clear.

Distribute copies of the resource sheet *Using hyphens for clarity* and ask pupils to read the sentences and to write an explanation for each. Discuss pupils' explanations, clarifying where necessary.

Resource sheet: Using hyphens for clarity

1	The slow moving people walked down the path.	The slow-moving people walked down the path.
2	We saw a man-eating shark on our holiday.	We saw a man eating shark on our holiday.
3	I have some little-used toys in my cupboard.	I have some little used toys in my cupboard.
4	There are four metre ropes in the school hall.	There are four-metre ropes in the school hall.

Support task

Distribute copies of the resource sheet *Match the meaning* and ask pupils to cut out the sentences and explanations and shuffle them. Pupils match each sentence to its meaning. Check their work for accuracy, discussing how the hyphens change the meaning of each sentence.

Resource sheet: Match the meaning

Sentences	Explanations
Thirty-odd children came to the party.	Approximately thirty children came to the party.
Thirty odd children came to the party.	Thirty strange children came to the party.
There was a child eating monster in the story.	A child eating a meal of monster in the story.
There was a child-eating monster in the story.	A story with a monster that eats children.
Six foot soldiers guarded the queen.	Six soldiers who fight on their feet guarded the queen.
Six-foot soldiers guarded the queen.	Soldiers who were sixfoot tall guarded the queen.

Extension task

Explain that in addition to joining compound nouns and compound adjectives, hyphens are also used to join other words. Display and discuss the following:

Compound verbs: to ice-skate

Numbers: twenty-one

Fractions: three-quarters

Discuss how hyphens are also sometimes used with some prefixes, such as 're-' (when meaning 'again'). Explain that not all words beginning with 're-' need a hyphen but there are occasions when hyphens are essential to guarantee the intended meaning, e.g. re-count. Read or display the following sentences.

1. The sofa needs recovering.
2. The star footballer has resigned.
3. I resent the email you wrote.
4. I used the iron to repress my shirt.

Ask pupils to use a dictionary to locate the definition of each word beginning with 're' and discuss the meaning of each sentence (e.g. The sofa needs finding.). Pupils should then rewrite each sentence, hyphenating the 're' words, and write an explanation of each sentence's new meaning.

Early finishers should use dictionaries to find definitions for: recreation / re-creation, reform / re-form, recall / re-call and reserve / re-serve.

Evaluating and improving writing 1 session

Ask pupils to read the resource sheet *Hyphens*, adding and removing hyphens so that it is punctuated correctly. When they have finished, they should discuss their answers, explaining why they have added or removed hyphens. Provide access to dictionaries to support pupils with this task.

Resource sheet: Hyphens

Josie, Gem and Georgie had been planning their ice skating trip for what felt like forever. In fact, they'd only started talking about it forty eight hours ago in Mrs Murphy's English lesson. It was always easy to have a good chat in one of Mrs Murphy's lessons as she liked to encourage the thirty odd children in the class to 'express their thoughts'. To say it was noisy in Mrs Murphy's lessons was an under-statement but it was perfect for an idle chit chat at the back of the room. And so, for the whole of the hour long lesson, the girls had sat on their high backed chairs and planned their trip to the ice rink.

The day of the ice skating trip arrived. Georgie's dad dropped them off out-side the ice rink and they rushed down the tunnel-like entrance to the reception desk. Josie asked the lady at the desk, "How much does it cost for three juniors?"

"Twenty four pounds," she replied.

Josie handed the money over and they went over to the benches to get ready. "Noooooo! I've left my ice skates in your dad's car," came the high-pitched exclamation from Gem. Her lip quivered: like she was going to cry.

Gem had re-signed herself to sitting on the side of the ice rink when she heard a familiar voice calling over to her. "Gem, I've got your skates. You left them in my car." It was Georgie's dad. Panic over and time to get ice skating.

Grammar in action: writing a persuasive text containing hyphens 1 session

Tell pupils they are going to write an advertisement for a computer game using a number of features, including hyphens and persuasive language. Ask them to recall features they may expect to find in persuasive writing (e.g. alliteration, exaggeration, rhetorical questions, the use of you / yours to address the audience). Ask them to think of compound adjectives that might persuade a reader to buy a product (e.g. top-quality, top-of-the-range, longer-lasting, state-of-the-art). Finally, ask pupils to identify different gaming genres (e.g. action, adventure, dancing, driving, fighting, platform, role-playing, sim (simulation), survival).

Use the resource sheet *Dancing with the cars* to model writing an advertisement, explaining to pupils that this advert is for a new type of game that combines two existing genres.

- Talk about the use of alliteration in the title and for the subheadings.
- Talk about the use of 'you' in the phrase 'Do you dare to dance and drive?'; discuss how this appeals directly to the reader, and how it is a rhetorical question.
- Draw attention to the use of hyphens to create compound nouns in dance-drive and mini-games.
- Model making choices and then changing them to reinforce how hyphens are used to form compound adjectives (e.g. genre-defying, action-packed).

After modelling, ask pupils to talk about gaming genres they could combine, the characteristics of these new genres and how they would promote such a game. Pupils should write their own game adverts making sure they include some compound nouns and adjectives. Ask them to check they have included hyphens where needed, including to avoid ambiguity. Challenge pupils to include hyphens to join numbers and compound verbs where appropriate.

Headings are used to separate sections of the text, which maintains cohesiveness. Further cohesiveness is created through the use of alliteration in each heading.

Italics are used to indicate that this is the name of the game.

Hyphen used to join numbers.

The use of a rhetorical question appeals directly to the reader.

As the ending mirrors the opening of the text, this is a further example of cohesiveness.

Resource sheet: Dancing with the cars

DO YOU DARE TO DANCE AND DRIVE?

A creative crossover

Dancing with the cars is the latest genre-defying game from Laser Games. This multi-player crossover combines the flair of dance gaming with the high-octane energy of driving games to create a whole new style of game: DANCE-DRIVE.

Endlessly entertaining

By using a combination of hand controls and dance steps, players navigate their way around twenty-five daring dance-inspired motor circuits. A host of additional challenges and mini-games mean that this action-packed game will keep players entertained for hours. Each racing circuit can be navigated solo or as a multi-player experience by sharing the fun with up to three friends.

Graphics and gameplay

State-of-the-art graphics and responsive gameplay will ensure that ***Dancing with the cars*** becomes the 'must-have' game for all fans of dancing and driving.

Do you dare to dance and drive?

Nouns are described with compound adjectives.

The hyphen indicates that Dance-drive is a noun.

Hyphen used to create a compound noun.

Certainty created through the use of the modal 'will'.

Learning outcome: to write a narrative recount using the past perfect form

Keywords: verb form, past participle, non-chronological, mythology, alliteration, personification, prologue

THE KING OF THE BIRDS

In Ireland, December 26th is called Wren Day (Lá an Dreoilín), and the tiny bird has always occupied a special place in Irish mythology. Although the wren is the smallest of birds, it is sometimes called the King of the Birds.

There is a song that begins, "The wren, the wren, the king of all birds..."

But how did such a tiny creature become the ruler of all the birds of the air?

In the still pre-dawn air, the bare frost-speckled winter trees were lined with birds.

Every glittering branch bowed beneath the weight of flocks that had gathered from all across Ireland, and the trees were alive with the whispering rasp of their feathers. The birds had kept to their own kin: the blackbirds and cuckoos clustered together, while the smaller birds – the sparrows, robins and thrushes, starlings, and swallows – swarmed the upper branches. The lower branches groaned beneath the weight of some of the bigger birds – the falcons and ospreys – while gulls, cormorants and the other seabirds moved across the hard-frozen earth, feet rasping on the thin covering of ice.

It was the winter solstice, the shortest day of the year, and the birds of Ireland had assembled to choose their ruler.

Boar, oxen, cats and dogs and even the deer had their rulers, but no one had claimed kingship over the birds, and for generations they had been ruled by a squabbling Parliament, mostly composed of black-eyed crows and nervous irritable robins. They could never agree on anything. Finally, the Parliament had turned to Relige, the ancient barn owl, for advice. No one knew how old he was. It was rumoured he had actually seen the birth of the world when it was pushed up from the ocean floor and that he had carried the first seeds to plant the great forests of oak, ash and yew that now blanketed the land. Even the fearsome two-legged humani acknowledged the owl's wisdom.

Relige had spent months flying from flock to flock, listening as each one claimed the right to rule. He knew if he simply picked a ruler it would solve nothing: the other bird flocks would not acknowledge them as their leader. Finally, he decided that the only way to choose a king would be by a trial of flight that would be open to all.

Thousands of sparrow messengers had flitted across the country carrying the news: the king would be chosen on the day of the winter solstice. Any birds interested in challenging for the leadership were to gather at Eo Munga, the Great Oak at the mouth of the River Shannon and one of the Five Sacred Trees of Ireland.

"Only a few will contest the kingship," Eala, one of the two snow-white swans, said to Relige. "A lot of the smaller birds will not even bother trying."

The swans, like the owl, had no interest in the kingship, and would act as judges.

"No, there will be more," Aela, her mate, said. "Everyone believes they can be the king."

"All the birds of Ireland will come," Relige said with a solemn nod. "If not to take part, then *tooo* observe and simply *tooo* be able to say that they were there when the king was chosen. Thousands will come," he hooted.

The day of the solstice dawned bitterly cold, the air from the ice lands at the top of the world carrying flecks of ice and the promise of snow. The birds started to gather just before the dawn. They arrived singly and in pairs, in long trailing V's across the grey sky or in huge wheeling flocks that moved as one.

Relige sat in the heart of the ancient Eo Mugna with all the flocks around, above and below him. He opened his huge eyes and blinked at the gathered birds. He had been right: there were thousands – *no*, there were tens of thousands gathered in the vast and ancient tree. The owl would referee the race and make sure that everyone observed the rule: to fly high and outlast all the others. But Relige, Eala and Aela were looking for more than strength and endurance. The king of the birds would have to be cunning and wise and, more importantly, would have to be respected by all the others.

The King of the Birds by Michael Scott

Links to the National Curriculum

Reading – comprehension

- maintain positive attitudes to reading and understanding of what they read by increasing their familiarity with a wide range of books, including myths, legends and traditional stories, modern fiction, fiction from our literary heritage, and books from other cultures and traditions
- discuss and evaluate how authors use language, including figurative language, considering the impact on the reader

Writing – composition

- draft and write by selecting appropriate grammar and vocabulary, understanding how such choices can change and enhance meaning

Writing – vocabulary, grammar and punctuation

- use the past perfect form of verbs to mark relationships of time and cause

TEACHING AND LEARNING IDEAS

Reading the text

1 session

Reading for meaning

Provide copies of the extract and read it aloud with pupils. Ask them to identify the genre (myth) and any features that indicate this (e.g. an explanation for the celebration of Wren Day; set in the distant past; contains talking animals). Ask questions about the use of techniques such as alliteration and personification (e.g. 'branch bowed beneath'; 'starlings, and swallows – swarmed'; 'The lower branches groaned'). Ask pupils to discuss the effectiveness of these techniques (e.g. they stimulate their senses of sound and vision).

Reading for grammar

Ask pairs of pupils to reread the prologue and story, identifying which part is set in the present and which part is set in the past (prologue present; story past). Explain that they are going to examine the author's use of different verb forms in this story to mark relationships of time.

Introduce the term 'past perfect', explaining that this verb form is created using the verb 'had' plus the 'past participle' of the main verb. Explain that the past participle often ends with '-ed' although there are many exceptions (e.g. 'had written').

Display the following examples:

had + past participle = past perfect

had + walked = had walked

had + written = had written

Challenge pupils to write five further examples of the past perfect using the model above. Review their answers, discussing any irregular forms of the past participle.

Ask pupils to reread the extract and to underline examples of the past perfect (e.g. '... the weight of flocks that had gathered ...' 'The birds had kept to their own kin ...').

Encourage pupils to check their answers in pairs. Review the task as a class.

Getting to grips with grammar

1 session

Independent task

Discuss how the past perfect shows events that happened before other events that also occurred in the past. Display the following:

Mrs Smith had told us a story before we went to assembly.

Mrs Smith (***had told*** us a story) before (we **went** to assembly).

(past perfect) (past)

Draw pupils' attention to the use of 'before' in the model sentence, explaining that this helps to establish the order of events. Ask them to think of five sentences that use 'before' in this way and to write them in their workbook. Encourage them to draw a timeline for each sentence and to annotate the events in their sentence as shown in the example (e.g. Mrs Jones had warned us to be on our best behaviour before we arrived at the museum).

Ask pupils to share their sentence and to explain the order of events.

Support task

Display the following sentence and ask pupils to use the past perfect form of the given verb to complete the sentence.

As I was leaving the house, mum asked if I ______________ (brush) my hair.

Check their answers, explaining that when using the past perfect, the answer is 'had brushed' as they need to use had + the past participle of the main verb.

Ask pupils to complete the resource sheet *Fill the gap* using the past perfect form of the verb provided in brackets. Once finished, they should check their work in pairs and write additional sentences, underlining the past perfect form.

Resource sheet: Fill the gap

1. Mr Brown asked if I ______________ (play) in the football team before.
2. When I called for Ravi, he was not at home. He ______________ (go) out.
3. I gave the rabbit some carrots because nobody else ______________ (feed) it yet.
4. Before we started the test, the teacher ______________ (explain) how to complete the answer sheet.
5. At the cinema, we ______________ (eat) all of the popcorn before the film started.

Extension task

Display the following sentence, asking pupils to identify the verb form describing Sam's doing (past perfect):

Sam had done a jigsaw before he went to school.

Discuss how the sentence describes a single event that finished (Sam doing the jigsaw) before something else took place (going to school).

Now display the following sentence:

Sam had been doing a jigsaw before he went to school.

Explain that in this sentence, Sam had been doing the jigsaw continuously and had then gone to school. This verb form is called the past perfect progressive and it is formed by using 'had', 'been' and the 'present participle' (-ing) to show that a past action was continuous up to another point in the past.

had + been + present participle = past perfect progressive

had + been + doing = had been doing

Distribute copies of the resource sheet *Different forms of past tense verbs*. Ask pupils to complete the verb table. Challenge them to add additional rows.

Resource sheet: Different forms of past tense verbs

Past simple	Past perfect	Past perfect progressive
	I had eaten the pizza.	
We drank the lemonade.		
		I had been painting a picture.

Evaluating and improving writing — 1 session

Provide pupils with copies of the resource sheet *Scrambled up!* Ask them to work in pairs to compare the two stories. They should explain which they think is more effective, giving reasons for their opinions. Listen to their thoughts and explain that both texts recount the story of Humpty Dumpty in non-chronological order and are good examples of a recount. You may want to discuss these points:

- Both stories use the past perfect form with the second story sometimes using a contracted form of 'had' (He'd done; they'd spent).
- Story 1 is told in a simple reverse chronological order whereas story 2 moves around from a point after the story, to the beginning and then back to the end again.
- Both stories use synonyms for 'earlier' (previously, before).
- Story 2 is embellished with additional information ('they'd spent many long nursery rhyme hours') and a simile ('just like firemen trying to coax a kitten out of a tree').
- Story 2 includes an example of the past perfect progressive ('had been working hard') which helps to show that they were working up to the point of the story being told.

Pupils should choose another nursery rhyme or traditional tale to retell in non-chronological order. They may find it helpful to write the rhyme in order on sentence strips and then rearrange them so that they can tell the story using the past perfect form.

Resource sheet: Scrambled up!

Story 1:
Humpty was at the bottom of the wall in pieces. Previously, all the King's horses and all the King's men had tried to put him together, but they couldn't. Humpty was at the bottom of the wall because he had fallen. Before he had fallen, Humpty had been sitting on the wall.

Story 2:
The King's horses and King's men had been working hard all day. They first knew it was going to be a long day when they heard that Humpty Dumpty had climbed to the top of the wall. He'd done this before and, just like firemen trying to coax a kitten out of a tree, they'd spent many long nursery rhyme hours climbing up the wall to bring him down safely. This time was different: Humpty had fallen. And no matter how hard they had tried, the King's horses and the King's men couldn't put Humpty together again.

Grammar in action: writing a narrative recount using the past perfect — 1 session

Explain to pupils that they are going to write a narrative recount using the past perfect form. Use the resource sheet *The alien in my bedroom* to model the process and features.

- Talk about how the opening of the story mirrors the prologue to *The King of the Birds* by using the present tense.
- Talk about how the past perfect has been formed ('I'd had a really good day ...', 'Mrs Roberts had given ...' etc.) and the use of 'I'd' to create an informal tone.
- Model thinking about word choices, drawing attention to alliteration in 'splendid story' and the use of inverted commas to show that these are Mrs Roberts' words.
- Model making verb choices and then changing them. Start by writing 'Walking up the stairs ..., stepped up the last stair, walked across the landing' and then discuss how the replacement verbs (climbing, skipped, bounded) have greater impact.

- Talk about how the phrase 'But before all of that' has been used to show the sequence of events and how cohesion has been created by reminding the reader that an alien had been left in the bedroom.

After modelling, ask pupils to think about what the alien could have done in the bedroom. Listen to their suggestions, encouraging them to phrase them using the past perfect form (e.g. 'The alien had drawn on my walls with …, she had taken all of my clothes out of the wardrobe ….').

Pupils should write their own story about an alien in their bedroom using the features modelled and their own list of ideas. Challenge the most able writers to include examples of the past perfect progressive in their writing (e.g. 'The alien had been washing …').

Resource sheet: The alien in my bedroom

Leaving an alien in your bedroom while you go to school is not to be recommended. Let me tell you why.

I'd had a really good day. Mrs Roberts had given me a house point for writing a 'splendid story', I'd scored a goal in our lunchtime football game and before that I'd swapped my cheese and chutney sandwich for James Arnold's chocolate chip cookie. But before all of that, I'd left an alien in my bedroom.

Climbing up the stairs, silently congratulating myself on my successes, I didn't notice the strange smell escaping from my room. I skipped up the last stair, bounded across the landing and flung open my bedroom door. In one instant all I could think was, 'Why had I left an alien in my bedroom?' …

The opening sentence is written in the present tense.

The use of 'I'd had' indicates the past perfect and demonstrates a shift in the tense of the text.

Precise verbs describe the action with clarity.

Personal pronouns indicate that the text is written in the first person.

The continued use of 'I'd' establishes an informal tone.

The repetition of 'I'd left an alien in my bedroom' ensures that the reader is reminded of earlier events.

Cohesion is created across the piece through the repeated reminders that an alien had been left in the bedroom.

Learning outcome: to use the present perfect form to write a fictional school report

Keywords: endurance, formality, passive voice, subject, past participle, Standard English, contractions

MYTHICAL CREATURES

Stories about the existence of mythical creatures have captured people's imaginations for thousands of years. Whether it's the reported discovery of one of Sasquatch's huge footprints in the American wilderness, a glimpse of the Yeti of the Himalayas or rumoured sightings of the Loch Ness Monster, it seems people just can't get enough of these larger-than-life creatures.

Sasquatch, the giant of the American wilderness

The legend of Sasquatch (or Bigfoot) has been told since people first lived on the continent of North America. Observers have described Sasquatch as a huge, ape-like man between 1.8 and 2.7m tall with an all-over-body covering of dark brown or black hair. His famous footprints have been reported to be a massive 60cm in length and 20cm wide.

Sasquatch has been sighted across the continent of North America, with most sightings taking place in the north-western states of the USA and in the area around the Great Lakes. Scientists have dismissed most sightings of Bigfoot as hoaxes or the misidentification of bears, which roam freely through many parts of North America.

The Yeti, the Abominable Snowman of the Himalayas

Like Sasquatch, the Yeti is said to be a huge ape-like creature, this time living in the mountainous region of the Himalayas. There have been sightings of a huge, hairy creature walking around the Himalayas for hundreds of years but interest in the creature gained popularity during the 20th century when Western mountaineers began exploring the region.

Whilst on these adventures, explorers took photographs they believed to be of the Yeti's footprints and collected samples of what they believed to be Yeti hair. Scientists have studied these photographs and samples for many years but have been unable to conclude that the Yeti exists. Despite this lack of scientific proof, the existence of the photographs and hair samples has ensured that the story of the Yeti continues to capture people's imaginations.

Nessie, the monster of the Loch

Stories about the Loch Ness Monster have been circulating since the 6th century AD, with the first recorded account having been made by the Abbot of Iona Abbey, Adamnán of Iona. Adamnán tells the story of a man swimming in the River Ness and being attacked by a water beast which dragged him below the water and drowned him. Adamnán's story goes on to explain how St Columba, a monk of Iona, then warned the water beast to go away and leave people alone, which it did. Nessie doubters have questioned the reliability of this story, pointing to the popularity of water-beast stories during mediaeval times and the fact that Adamnán's story was written 100 years after the events he described.

The popularity of the Nessie story increased during the 1930s, which was in part due to improved access to the remote Highlands area (meaning more people were able to visit Loch Ness) and the increasing availability of cameras. Several sightings had referred to a reptilian or dinosaur-like creature with a small head and long neck, and photographs taken in the 1930s seemed to confirm this. However, in recent years, photography experts have dismissed these photographs as fakes. Despite this, the image of a huge reptilian creature with a small head and long neck has endured.

In 2017 alone, there were eight recorded sightings of the Loch Ness Monster, including one by nine-year-old Sam Knight. Sam had taken hundreds of photographs whilst on holiday on Loch Ness. It was only when his family returned home that they found a photograph showing what appeared to be a fin rising from the Loch. Sam's photograph was examined by experts who were unable to dismiss it as a fake. Sam's photograph has now been added to the growing bank of evidence that there is something strange living in Loch Ness.

These are just a few of the stories that exist across the world about strange creatures seemingly from a different time and place. Whether you believe the stories or not, what connects them all is how they have endured, despite continued efforts to disprove them and limited amounts of scientific evidence. People, it seems, simply can't get enough of stories about larger-than-life creatures.

Mythical Creatures by Rachel Clarke

Links to the National Curriculum

Reading – comprehension

- maintain positive attitudes to reading and understanding of what they read by continuing to read and discuss an increasingly wide range of fiction, poetry, plays, non-fiction and reference books or textbooks
- understand what they read by identifying how language, structure and presentation contribute to meaning

Writing – composition

- plan their writing by identifying the audience for and purpose of the writing, selecting the appropriate form and using other similar writing as models for their own
- evaluate and edit by proposing changes to vocabulary, grammar and punctuation to enhance effects and clarify meaning

Writing – vocabulary, grammar and punctuation

- use the present perfect form of verbs to mark relationships of time and cause

TEACHING AND LEARNING IDEAS

Reading the text

1 session

Reading for meaning

Distribute copies of the extract and read it aloud with pupils. Check that they know the location of North America, the Himalayas and Loch Ness. Talk about the purpose of the text (it is written to explain beliefs people hold about mythical creatures and how different evidence has been used to support or discount these beliefs). Ask pupils to share their understanding of how the word 'mythical' is used in this text, establishing that it is used to describe creatures that many people believe exist, but where there is no definitive evidence to support this belief. Ask pupils whether they believe in the existence of the mythical creatures and which information in the text leads them to this conclusion. Ask them to define 'endure' and to consider why stories about mythical creatures have endured for such a long time.

Reading for grammar

Tell pupils that they will be analysing the extract to learn how different verb forms show different relationships of time. Display the following sentences:

'Stories about the existence of mythical creatures <u>captured</u> people's imaginations for thousands of years.'

'Stories about the existence of mythical creatures <u>have captured</u> people's imaginations for thousands of years.'

Ask pupils to discuss the meaning of the sentences. Explain that the first sentence shows that at one point in the past stories captured peoples' interest for thousands of years but no longer do. The second sentence shows that stories captured their interest for thousands of years and still do. Establish that the first sentence uses the past simple form of 'captured' and the second sentence uses the present perfect 'have captured'. This second form shows how an action took place in the past and has continued up to recent time. Display the following example:

have / has + past participle = present perfect

have + captured = have captured

has + captured = has captured

Clarify that have / has are used depending on the subject the verb is being joined to. For example:

<u>The story has</u> captured people's imaginations. (singular subject: story)

<u>The stories have</u> captured people's imaginations. (plural subject: stories)

Ask pupils to reread the extract, underlining examples of the present perfect in a colour of their choice.

Display the following sentence:

'Stories about the Loch Ness Monster <u>have been circulating</u> since the 6th century AD.'

Explain that the underlined phrase is a verb form called the 'present perfect progressive'. It is a verb form that uses the present participle '-ing' to show that an event or action is continuous. Display the following example:

have / has + been + present participle = present perfect progressive

have + been + circulating = have been circulating

has + been + circulating = has been circulating

Ask pupils to underline this on their copies of the text in a different colour to the one used earlier.

Independent task

Explain to pupils that they are going to practise forming the present perfect and present perfect progressive by writing true and false statements.

Display the following sentence stems:

I've never ....

I have been .... this week / today, etc.

I haven't ever ....

Explain to pupils that they are going to use the sentence stems to write two truthful sentences and one untruthful sentence. Model with the following examples:

I've never travelled on an aeroplane.

I have been jumping on my bed a lot this week.

I haven't ever completed my homework.

They should then read their sentences aloud and ask a partner to guess which is the lie. Explain that their partner may ask additional questions to establish which sentences are true and false. When pupils have guessed each other's lies, they should write all the sentences in their books, underline the verb forms and indicate whether each is present perfect or present perfect progressive. Pupils should swap partners, write new statements and repeat the game.

Support task

Display the sentence: 'I played with the dog.'

Ask pupils to rewrite the sentence in the present perfect and present perfect progressive (I have played with the dog. I have been playing with the dog.)

Ask pupils to underline the verb form in each sentence. They should then complete the resource sheet *Present perfect and present perfect progressive* by re-writing each sentence using the present perfect and the present perfect progressive.

Resource sheet: Present perfect and present perfect progressive

1. Jo skipped to school this morning.
2. The cat climbed the tree.
3. The children played football.
4. Mum and Dad planned the summer holiday.
5. Asif read his book.

Extension task

Read or display the following sentences, asking pupils to identify whether they use the present perfect or present perfect progressive:

1. Sam has been jumping on a trampoline.
2. The cat's been chasing the dog again.
3. Zoe and Nadia have been playing chess.
4. We've been playing football all afternoon.

Listen to their responses, clarifying that all the sentences use the present perfect progressive. Draw attention to the use of the contracted form of 'has' and 'have' in sentences 2 and 4, clarifying that these are still examples of the present perfect progressive.

Display the following topics: singing in the choir; telling lies; playing football; reading a book; winning a medal. Ask pupils to write sentences about each topic using the present perfect progressive and contracted forms of 'have' and 'has' (e.g. I've been singing in the school choir since I was in Year 3).

Pupils should then devise their own topics and sentences to show how contractions can be used in the present perfect progressive (e.g. We've been getting a lot of homework from our teacher).

Evaluating and improving writing 1 session

Provide pupils with copies of the resource sheet *Postcard from the seaside* and ask them to read it. Discuss how the limited writing space on a postcard prompts the abbreviated style and that the informality is appropriate (e.g. the use of 'Love and hugs' and 'Phew!'). Ask pupils to model reading the postcard as it is written and then how it could be rephrased using full sentences. Listen to some of their responses.

Now ask them to rewrite the postcard as a letter. They should maintain an informal tone and consider using contracted forms, but must write in full sentences. Remind pupils that some of the events have only recently been completed and that some are ongoing at the time of writing the postcard. This means they will need to use the present perfect and present perfect progressive to describe those events, but that some events such as 'Had pizza for tea last night' will require the use of the simple past.

Resource sheet: Postcard from the seaside

Dear Granny,

Hope you're well. Been here four days – absolutely brilliant. Have played on beach every day. Been swimming twice. Had pizza for tea last night. Fish and chips out of paper today. Have you done that?

Not used binoculars you gave me yet. Put them in my backpack – will use them tomorrow at Nature Reserve.

Dog's been chasing seagulls – not caught any yet. Phew!

Missing Grandpa's bad jokes.

See you soon.

Love and hugs,

Peter xxx

Place stamp here

Mrs M Ward,
3 Leaf Lane,
Sunnyborough
SB9 3ZX

Grammar in action: writing a school report using the present perfect form of verbs 1 session

Tell pupils they are going to write a school report using present perfect forms of verbs. Establish that they should include sections for each subject, summaries of what has been taught and descriptions of the pupil's achievements. Explain that school reports are formal documents, meaning pupils' full names and Standard English are used, and contracted forms of words are avoided. Use the resource sheet *End-of-year report* to model writing an extract from a school report.

- Talk about the use of 'has been learning' to indicate William's continuous learning and how 'opportunity' in the phrase 'he had the opportunity' is more formal than writing 'chance'.
- Discuss the word choices, drawing attention to 'impressive' and 'enthusiastic' to help create an impression of William as a talented, hard-working student.
- Show how different grammatical structures alter the focus of sentences by writing 'and has drawn a very impressive cross-sectional drawing of how the Romans used different materials to build roads' before changing it to the passive to emphasise the materials used rather than the builders.
- Demonstrate making choices about verb forms by changing them from simple to perfect forms (e.g. 'has played' suggests that William is no longer playing tag rugby, whereas 'has been playing tag rugby' shows that William continues to play tag rugby).

After modelling, ask pupils to plan and write their own fictional school reports.

Resource sheet: End-of-year report

HISTORY

This year in History, William has been learning about life in Britain during the time of the Roman Empire. He has found out about life in the Roman army and on our trip to the fort he had the opportunity to dress up as a Roman centurion. He has learned about Roman road building and has drawn a very impressive cross-sectional drawing of the materials used by the Roman road builders. William enjoyed our trip to the Roman villa. Since the visit, he has designed and made a beautiful mosaic, which the headteacher has displayed in the school entrance hall. William has clearly enjoyed History this year and it has been a pleasure to teach such an enthusiastic young man.

PE

In PE, William has been playing tag rugby. He has tried hard and has worked well as part of a team. He has shown great skill in catching and throwing a rugby ball, but has struggled to grab other players' tags. I have enjoyed teaching William for PE and am sure that he has enjoyed the lessons.

The phrase 'he had the opportunity' is more formal than writing 'he had the chance'.

The passive voice puts the emphasis on the materials used rather than the builders. Discuss the different emphasis if this was written as 'and has drawn a very impressive cross-sectional drawing of how the Romans used different materials to build roads'.

The use of the present perfect progressive 'has been learning' indicates William's continuous learning.

Discuss word choices, drawing attention to 'impressive' and 'enthusiastic' to help create an impression of William as a talented, hard-working student.

The use of 'has been playing tag rugby' shows that William continues to play tag rugby. If this had been written as 'has played' it would suggest that he is no longer playing tag rugby.

Learning outcome: to write a menu for an ice-cream parlour using expanded noun phrases

Keywords: non-finite clause, prepositional phrase, relative clause, modify, object, adjectival phrase, expanded noun phrase

SELIM-HASSAN the SEVENTH

Selim-Hassan the Seventh lived in Pushnapanjipetal, which is and was famous for nothing at all, except for the extreme hairiness of all the men who lived there. Selim-Hassan's father was the village barber. Every day he soaped and lathered and foamed the beards of the men of the village and then, with eight swift swoops of his shining silver razor, shaved them so smoothly that their skin felt like the softest silk.

"Look in the mirror," Selim-Hassan's father would say. And the customer would peer at himself in Selim-Hassan's splendid gilt-edged mirror, decorated with golden roses, and nod.

"You are right, Selim-Hassan the Sixth. It is indeed the finest shave that I have ever had."

Selim-Hassan's grandfather had been a barber. So also had his great-grandfather, his great-great-grandfather and his great-great-great-grandfather. Each of them in turn had practised and refined the art of shaving from twelve swift swoops of the shining razor to eleven, from eleven to ten, from ten to nine. Each of them in turn had passed on their skills and knowledge to their grateful oldest son.

Selim-Hassan the Seventh was different. He did *not* want to be a barber. He was not in the least grateful when his father showed him how to sharpen the razors on a wetted stone. He was not at all grateful when he was given the opportunity to sweep up the curls and whiskers on the shop floor. He was positively rude when a customer asked him to pass him a hot towel.

Selim-Hassan's father grew anxious. "Could it be," he asked Selim-Hassan's mother, "that our son takes after his great-great-great-great-grandfather?"

Selim-Hassan's mother rolled her eyes. "I pray that it isn't so," she said.

Selim-Hassan's great-great-great-great-grandfather, the first Selim Hassan, had been a pirate. He had sailed the oceans of the world wrecking ships and collecting thousands of shiny objects so that he could see his reflection any time he felt the need. It was Selim-Hassan's great-great-great-great-grandfather who had brought the splendid gilt-edged mirror, decorated with golden roses, back to the village in a treasure chest, together with the silver razors. He never used the razors; he spent his days admiring his wonderfully luxuriant black and curly beard in the splendid gilt-edged mirror and singing loud piratical songs.

When Selim-Hassan the Seventh began to ask questions about this less than illustrious ancestor, his father shook his head. "He was not a man to be proud of," Selim-Hassan the Sixth said firmly. "It is not a good thing to be a thief. You, my son, will not be like him. Our family has been waiting for you for seven generations. You will be famous for being the first among us ever to achieve the perfect shave with only seven swift swoops of the silver razor." And Selim-Hassan the Sixth smiled hopefully at the Seventh.

Selim-Hassan the Seventh shuffled his feet and said nothing. He found his lessons in soaping and lathering and foaming tedious. He much preferred to slip away and play marbles with his friends under the shady palm trees by the well.

Selim-Hassan the Seventh by Vivian French

Links to the National Curriculum

Reading – comprehension

- maintain positive attitudes to reading and understanding of what they read by increasing their familiarity with a wide range of books, including myths, legends and traditional stories, modern fiction, fiction from our literary heritage, and books from other cultures and traditions
- understand what they read by identifying how language, structure and presentation contribute to meaning

Writing – composition

- plan their writing by identifying the audience for and purpose of the writing, selecting the appropriate form and using other similar writing as models for their own
- draft and write by selecting appropriate grammar and vocabulary, understanding how such choices can change and enhance meaning

Writing – vocabulary, grammar and punctuation

- use expanded noun phrases to convey complicated information concisely

TEACHING AND LEARNING IDEAS

Reading the text

1 session

Reading for meaning

Provide copies of the extract and read it aloud with pupils. Seek opinions about whether the story is serious or light-hearted and what makes them think this (e.g. it's light-hearted as it's about hairy men; the long lists of 'great' sound quite humorous). Ask pupils what they know about the use of 'seven' in stories, eliciting that it is often used as a magical or significant number. Ask pupils to predict what this might mean for Selim-Hassan (e.g. he may have special powers; he may do something amazing).

Ask pupils which objects are important to Selim-Hassan the Sixth's work (razors and mirror). Talk about authors often placing important objects and information at the beginning of a story in order to use them later on. Ask them to predict which of these objects will prove important in the story and why they think this (e.g. the mirror because it is mentioned frequently and in great detail).

Reading for grammar

Tell pupils they are going to learn about the author's use of noun phrases in this text to convey complicated information concisely. Display the following sentence:

'Every day he soaped and lathered and foamed the beards of the men of the village …'

Ask pupils to identify the object of the sentence (the beards). Highlight this, reminding them that it is a noun phrase. Ask pupils to identify what other information is given about the beards (they belong to the men of the village). Underline 'the beards of the men of the village', explaining that this is a noun phrase as all the information is about the beards. Provide pupils with the prepositions 'with' and 'on' and ask them to use these words to modify the phrase 'the beards' (e.g. the beards with curly whiskers; the beards on the faces of the men).

Display the following sentence:

'It was Selim-Hassan's great-great-great-great-grandfather who had brought the splendid gilt-edged mirror, decorated with golden roses, back to the village in a treasure chest, together with the silver razors.'

Ask pupils to identify what this sentence tells them about the appearance of the mirror. Underline the information about the mirror ('<u>the splendid gilt-edged mirror, decorated with golden roses</u>'). Clarify that 'mirror' is a noun, and that the underlined information describes it. All the underlined information is an expanded noun phrase.

Explain that this expanded noun phrase is made up of an adjectival phrase ('splendid gilt-edged') and a subordinate clause (a non-finite clause) that provides more information about the mirror: 'decorated with golden roses'. Explain that sometimes clauses that start with the -ed or -ing form of a verb are used to give more information about a noun. In this sentence, the verb 'decorate' is used at the beginning of a clause to give more information about the mirror.

Provide pupils with the verbs 'painted', 'coloured', 'constructed' and 'fashioned'. In pairs, ask them to modify the phrase 'the splendid gilt-edged mirror' by adding non-finite clauses beginning with these words (e.g. the splendid gilt-edged mirror, painted green and purple).

List their responses and underline the non-finite clauses.

Independent task

Explain to pupils that they are going to write expanded noun phrases that can be used as clues about famous people, characters or places. Each clue must include either a prepositional phrase or a non-finite clause after the noun. They should also consider whether to include adjectival phrases for extra detail. For example:

I am a hairy-faced baddie, with big teeth, big eyes and a big nose. (the Big Bad Wolf)

This is a huge metal tower, reaching skywards above Paris. (the Eiffel Tower)

When they have written their clues, pupils should share them in pairs for solving. They should suggest improvements to each other's clues to make the descriptions as clear as possible. Check pupils' work, asking them to identify where they have used non-finite clauses and prepositional phrases.

Support task

Distribute the resource sheet *Noun phrases*. Ask pupils to cut out and shuffle the phrases and then match the noun phrases and prepositional phrases. They should then consider how to improve each sentence by adding further descriptive information (e.g. The mirror with a border – The shiny mirror with a flowery gold border).

Resource sheet: Noun phrases

Noun phrases	Prepositional phrases
The mirror	with a border
A post box	in the street
The car	with wheels
The block of flats	over the road
The treasure	in the chest
The bench	under the tree
A razor	with a handle

Extension task

Tell pupils they are going to use relative clauses, prepositional phrases and non-finite clauses to create expanded noun phrases. Ask them to read the first sentence of the extract and to locate the phrase that tells them about the men of Pushnapanjipetal ('the extreme hairiness of all the men who lived there'). Talk about the amount of detail in the phrase, establishing that the noun phrase 'the men' is expanded by the noun phrase 'extreme hairiness', the preposition 'of' and the relative clause 'who lived there'.

Display the phrase 'The three new kittens …'. Show pupils how it can be modified with a relative clause (e.g. The three new kittens who were tiny and fluffy).

Remind pupils that relative clauses are introduced with who, whom, whose, which, that, where and when.

Provide pupils with a number of noun phrases (e.g. the school, a parcel, the boy, a car, a castle, the dog, a lamp, a school, some trees, the zoo) and ask them to expand each with adjectives, prepositional phrases, non-finite clauses and relative clauses. For example:

The boy

The young boy

The young boy with blonde hair

The young boy, dressed to impress

The young boy, who has blonde hair

Evaluating and improving writing 1 session

Provide pupils with copies of the resource sheet *Traffic report*. Ask them to read the passage and then recount the events and appearance of each vehicle orally to a partner. Explain that they are to rewrite the passage more concisely. Demonstrate this by rewriting the first two sentences as:

A crash took place earlier today at the crossroads just outside town.

Explain that the prepositional phrase 'just outside town' removes the need to write 'the crossroads are just', making the description more concise. Talk about the traffic report, encouraging pupils to model possible noun phrases such as 'a blue soft-top Mercedes with silver alloy wheels … a white Mini decorated with a union jack'.

Pupils should now rewrite the account more concisely using expanded noun phrases to help them.

Resource sheet: Traffic report

A crash took place earlier today at the crossroads. The crossroads are just outside town. Four vehicles were involved in the accident. The first vehicle was a blue car: a Mercedes. It had a soft top and silver alloy wheels. It bumped into a white car which had a union jack painted on the roof. This car was a Mini. The bonnet of the Mini was dented, causing steam to rise from it. The third vehicle was a bus. The bus was brand new and had only just left the factory where it was built. The final vehicle was a motorcycle. It was a vintage model and had a sidecar. The motorcycle avoided hitting the other vehicles. This was due to the expertise of its driver. It appears that she is a trained stuntwoman.

Witnesses report that the accident was caused by the person driving the Mercedes. Witnesses say that he was talking on his mobile phone whilst driving. No-one was injured in the accident. The accident has now been cleared.

Grammar in action: using noun phrases to write a menu 1 session

Explain to pupils that they are going to design and write a menu for an ice-cream parlour. They will need to think of a name for their ice-cream parlour, write a welcoming introduction and create a list of food and drink that is available. Ask pupils to think of categories of food and drink they would expect to find in an ice-cream parlour (e.g. cones and wafers; sundaes; frozen yoghurts and sorbets; milkshakes; soft and fizzy drinks). Explain that they don't need to include all of these categories, but they should think of at least three dishes for each category that they do choose. Model writing part of an ice-cream parlour menu using the resource sheet *Frosty's Ice-cream Parlour.*

- Draw pupils' attention to the noun phrase 'the only award-winning ice-cream parlour in town'.
- Discuss ways to introduce the items in the 'cones and wafers' section, talking about the use of 'crunchy' as an adjective and as an alliterative tool.
- Talk about how 'ice cream with strawberry sauce and a wafer' is made to sound more delicious by expanding the nouns and using a non-finite clause to describe how the sauce is added to the ice cream. Then talk about using a preposition to add information about the wafer. Continue in this way as you model writing the rest of the 'Cones and wafers' menu items.
- Discuss the closing statement on the menu, explaining that a flurry is something that moves quickly and lightly like snow which makes it a good word to use on an ice-cream menu, and that some ice cream is whipped, which makes 'whip up' another good phrase to use.

You may want to find some print and television food adverts to show pupils how expanded noun phrases are used to advertise food (e.g. https://www.youtube.com/watch?v=EHFKE6PD_6U).

Resource sheet: Frosty's Ice-cream Parlour

<u>Welcome to Frosty's Ice-cream Parlour</u>

Frosty's ice-cream parlour uses the best locally sourced ingredients to bring you the only award-winning ice cream in town. Our menu is filled with delicious treats that will keep you coming back to Frosty's time and time again.

<u>Cones and wafers</u>

Choose from our delicious range of crunchy cones and wafers.

- Fresh vanilla ice cream served with strawberry sauce and a crispy toffee wafer
- Two large scoops of chocolate ice cream in a handmade caramel cone
- One slice of Frosty's special recipe Neapolitan ice cream sandwiched between two chocolate wafers

If you can't see what you like on the menu, just ask and we'll whip up your favourite in a flurry.

Acknowledgements

The author and publisher are grateful to the copyright holders for permission to use quoted material. Every effort has been made to trace copyright holders and obtain their permission for the use of copyright material. The author and publisher will gladly receive information enabling them to rectify any error or omission in subsequent editions.

Illustrations © Shutterstock.com

Text © 2016 Francesca Armour-Chelu.
FENN HALFLIN AND THE FEARZERO by Francesca Armour-Chelu
Reproduced by permission of Walker Books Ltd, London SE11 5HJ
www.walker.co.uk
Superstructures: Fabulous Bridges by Ian Graham reproduced by permission of Franklin Watts, an imprint of Hachette Children's Books, Carmelite House, 50 Victoria Embankment, London EC4Y 0DZ
King of the Birds: Beyond the Start by Michael Scott © Michael Scott, 2014. Published by HarperCollins Children's Books. Used by permission
'If I Were King' taken from *When We Were Very Young* by A.A. Milne. Text copyright © The Trustees of the Pooh Properties 1924. Published by Egmont UK Ltd and used with permission of Egmont UK Ltd and Curtis Brown Ltd.
Selim-Hassan the Seventh. Reprinted by permission of HarperCollins Publishers Ltd
© (2008) (Vivian French)
Black Holes. Reprinted by permission of HarperCollins Publishers Ltd
© (2013) (Anna Claybourne)
'*The Stick Book*' by Fiona Danks and Jo Schofield published by Frances Lincoln www.goingwild.net'. Used by permission

Published by Keen Kite Books
An imprint of HarperCollins*Publishers* Ltd
1 London Bridge Street
London
SE1 9GF

10 9 8 7 6 5 4 3 2 1

ISBN 978-0-00-829527-1

British Library Cataloguing in Publication Data

A catalogue record for this publication is available from the British Library.

Author: Rachel Clarke
Series Editor: Rachel Clarke
Commissioning Editor: Shelley Teasdale
Project Management: Shelley Teasdale and Fiona Watson
Editor: Fiona Watson
Cover Design: Anthony Godber
Internal design: QBS Learning